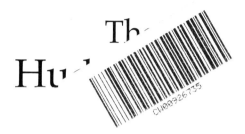

The
Hu~
Kirkbur ~ Branch

by
J.N. Fisher

THE OAKWOOD PRESS

© Oakwood Press & J.N. Fisher 1997

British Library Cataloguing in Publication Data
A Record for this book is available from the British Library
ISBN 0 85361 510 1

Typeset by Oakwood Graphics.
Repro by Ford Graphics, Ringwood, Hants.
Printed by Alpha Print (Oxford) Ltd, Witney, Oxon.

Undated picture of the Yorkshire County Cricket side featuring Wilfred Rhodes (*third from left, back row*) and George Herbert Hirst (*first left, middle row*), 'sons' of Kirkheaton.
Author's Collection

Title Page: The 1921 winners plaque for the LNWR North Eastern Division station garden competition. *National Railway Museum*

Published by
The Oakwood Press
P.O. Box 13, Usk, Mon., NP5 1YS.

Contents

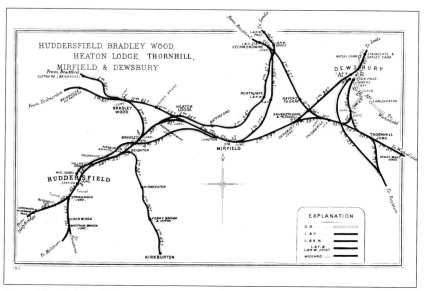

Map of the Huddersfield area in 1914, clearly showing the Kirkburton branch.
Author's Collection

3

Introduction

This book aims to tell the story of the branch railway which operated between Huddersfield and the township of Kirkburton, in the West Riding of Yorkshire. It was the only London & North Western Railway (LNWR) branch in an area where Lancashire & Yorkshire Railway (L&YR) branches proliferated.

After receiving Parliamentary approval in 1863 the branch opened for passengers in 1867, just 20 years after the railway first reached Huddersfield. The passenger service was, though, relatively short-lived and ceased, apart from specials and excursions, in 1930.

Goods services continued over the whole of the branch for a further 35 years and over a truncated section for 6 years beyond that.

The journey between Huddersfield and Kirkburton totalled just over 6 miles, with the branch line itself being 4½ miles long. In addition to the two terminal stations, there were three other stations along the line at Deighton, Kirkheaton and Fenay Bridge and Lepton. Reflecting the line's industrial connection a temporary halt was constructed during World War I for workers at British Dyes. The journey time was about 20 minutes.

Although constructed and operated as a branch it was originally intended as a through route to Barnsley and the Yorkshire coalfield. The branch stations tended to be somewhat remote from the communities they were intended to serve and undoubtedly this was a major factor in the early demise of the passenger service.

Little of the euphoria which seemed to surround the construction and opening of many branch lines appears to have been prevalent with this branch, indeed the London & North Western Railway Company had no intention of having an official opening ceremony. Local people and the contractors felt differently, though, as will be seen from the main text.

It was perhaps in its service to industry where the benefits of the branch were most in evidence. In addition to carrying raw materials in for local industry, and manufactured goods out the railway connected directly to a number of private sidings and even fully fledged industrial railway systems. It was one of these which kept a section of the branch open for a further six years after closure of the remainder, and which may yet lead to the re-opening of a section. In this regard interest in the branch has already been re-kindled with the re-opening of a passenger station at Deighton, originally the first station on the branch after leaving Huddersfield.

All railway branch lines have an interesting story to tell, revolutionising as they did a way of life by providing the first realistic means of mass transport, and hopefully the Kirkburton branch is no exception to this.

Chapter One

Description of the Area

According to *Place Names in the West Riding* by F.W. Moorman, the origin of the name of Kirkburton is slightly indeterminate, but it makes the following observations:

Most of the English Burtons go back to Burton; a Manor House enclosure, but probably not with Kirkburton. Domesday Book spelling Bertone associates it with Bere (Barley); the barley enclosure or barley field, and identified it with various English Bartons. But the form Byrton and Birton seems to connect the place with Byre; cowhouse, byre, which would give us Byretun, Byrton; an enclosure of land with a cow house upon it, as the original form of the name. The prefixing with Kirk dates from the reign of Edward III (1327-1371) when a church was built at Kirkburton.

In regard to Kirkheaton, the same book states:

Domesday Book spelling Heptone connects Kirkheaton with Hepton - but probably an incorrect form. Heaton is almost certainly identical with Heaton in Earl's Heaton and comes from heah, hea; high and tun; an enclosure. Kirkheaton accordingly means an enclosure of land on high ground with a church.

Geographically Kirkburton is located 5 miles south-east of Huddersfield. Little appears to be known about the history of the district until medieval times, although there are records of ancient British, Roman and Norman encampments on nearby Castle Hill. These records indicate that the site carried a hill fort of Brigantean origin. Between 56 BC and AD 43 the summit was surrounded by two ditches and banks and, for part of the way, with a third ditch. Within this fort Cartamondua, the queen of the Brigantes, had her citadel. After the defeat of the Brigantean leader, Venutius, in AD 74 the citadel was destroyed by fire, but the ramparts and ditches remained, as they still do, as a monument to the landscape.

The site was again used between the 11th and 13th centuries but no modifications were made to the profile of the hill and its ramparts. Today Castle Hill remains as a dominant feature and a landmark for Huddersfield and surrounding districts. A stone tower was constructed to commemorate the diamond jubilee of the reign of Queen Victoria.

At one time the Kirkburton district was a dense forest, probably with a heavy bog in the lower areas, and was home to many wild animals. With the coming of the Romans the British tribes in the north, which were probably Parisi and Brigantes, were driven away from the more fertile parts and took refuge in the mountainous foothills. No trace of them now remains, however.

There are also a few traces of Saxon influence though the churches at Kirkheaton and Kirkburton are reputed to have been established from the Mother Church, founded by St Paulinus at Dewsbury, and these villages were the early centres of development in the area.

Shop Lane, Kirkheaton c. 1905. A little girl watches as a woman buys from the carrier's cart.

The present church at Kirkheaton is over 600 years old being built in the reign of Edward III (1327-1377). Parish registers commenced in 1540. The church has a tower 78 ft high, restoration taking place in 1850, 1871 and 1907/8. Kirkburton church also has its roots in the 14th century but the bulk of it was destroyed by fire in 1886. The only portions escaping damage were the chantry of the Blessed Virgin Mary and the tower.

Industrial development in the Kirkburton area commenced with the textile industry at the end of the 18th century, which was at the beginning of the Industrial Revolution. Cloth was, however, manufactured in the district prior to this time but this was largely in homes as a family activity. Huddersfield is in the 'textile zone' of the West Riding of Yorkshire and in spite of the reduced size of this industry it remains even today as a centre for fine worsted.

Other industries prevalent in the Kirkburton and Huddersfield area include agriculture, coal mining, engineering, quarrying and the manufacture of fireworks.

Collieries were numerous in the Huddersfield area with the following being listed as working in the vicinity of Kirkburton in 1861:

Colliery	Owner
Kirkburton	W. Rhodes
Kirkheaton	Messrs Cardwells
Rowley	Copley and Co.
Whiteley (Kirkheaton)	Matthews and Co.

Quarrying is evident in many parts of the Huddersfield area. The industry grew with the housing and mill demands during the late 18th and early 19th century, when railway works, stations and bridges were wanting a good quality of stone.

An interesting industry associated with the area was the production of explosives and fireworks with no less than six factories at the height of production. These tended to be concentrated around the Lepton and Fenay Bridge areas, with perhaps the best known being Lion Fireworks which opened in 1906. They were to provide a good deal of goods traffic for the railway which was handled in the sidings at Fenay Bridge and Lepton station. During World War I it was estimated that 4 million hand grenades were despatched annually from the station.

From a transport point of view the Huddersfield area was well served by packhorse roads and subsequently by coaches for the conveyance of passengers. The conveyance of goods was given a considerable boost, however, by the construction of the Ramsden canal between Cooper Bridge, where it joined the Calder and Hebble Navigation, and Huddersfield. The canal opened in 1780, after the Bill authorising its construction had been given Royal Assent on 9th March, 1774. The canal was named after Sir John Ramsden (1775-1839), who conceived the idea, and cost £11,974 14s. 4d. to construct. It has a total length of 3¾ miles, rising some 93 feet through locks 15 ft wide. An interesting item in the list of expenditure was 'Deighton township for damage 6s. 0d'. This was to be the future location for the first station on the Kirkburton railway. Ultimately the canal was to be extended into Lancashire as the Huddersfield Narrow Canal. This was a spectacular construction between Huddersfield and Ashton-under-Lyne. It climbed to a summit of 646 feet via 42 locks, and included in its journey the 5,451 yds-long Standedge tunnel.

From a Local Government point of view Kirkburton is currently administered as part of the Kirklees Metropolitan Council. This council was established at Local Government re-organisation in 1974. It is centred on Huddersfield and is one of five districts which make up the Metropolitan County of West Yorkshire. Prior to this the unit of Local Government was the Urban District of Kirkburton which covered an area of 13,890 acres in the south-west part of the West Riding of Yorkshire. The Urban District consisted of a number of villages amalgamated for administrative purposes taking its name from the village of Kirkburton. The district is on the edge of the Pennines which rise to 1,200 feet within the area of the Urban District. At the 1952 census the population of the Urban District was 17,800, of these 11,106 were electors. The Urban District was inaugurated in 1938, the village previously being administered by Kirkburton Council. This latter Council purchased a building on the 4th December, 1935 for use as a Town Hall for the sum of £900, subsequently opening as a Town Hall on 27th August, 1938. It was formerly a house set in its own grounds and is located near to the site of the railway station.

Situated close to the Pennines the area generally supports a large number of reservoirs. Huddersfield built two small reservoirs in 1827 and 1828, and then two larger ones in 1836 and 1838. During the period 1870 to 1875 five more reservoirs were built, authorised by the Huddersfield Waterworks Act in 1869. Further building followed in 1937, all these developments being supported by a large number of boreholes sunk to tap the reserves of underground water.

Huddersfield and district can boast many sporting successes. The Huddersfield Town Football Club was the first club ever to top the First Division of the Football League for three successive seasons in the late 1920s. Rugby League football was founded in the town and there have always been strong cricketing traditions. Kirkheaton was the birthplace of two of Yorkshire and England's greatest cricketers. George Herbert Hirst was born in the village on 7th September, 1871 and Wilfred Rhodes on 29th October, 1877.

The textile trade experienced a tragic fire in 1818 when 17 females aged 9 to 18 died whilst working through the night behind locked doors in a factory at Colnebridge. Their remains are interred in one grave in Kirkheaton churchyard alongside a memorial which reads 'a striking and awful instance of the uncertainty of life'.

Finally on 10th September, 1932 the *Huddersfield Examiner* included the following comments being the recollection of a former Kirkheaton man, Mr Hiram Hardcastle, aged 87 years:

> Perhaps 80 years ago a carrier's cart used to run regularly once or twice a week from Huddersfield through . . . Kirkburton . . . to Clayton West . . . The cart was pulled by two great St Bernard dogs.

Chapter Two

The Railway Reaches Huddersfield

The railway came to Huddersfield on 2nd August, 1847 with the official opening of the line between Cooper Bridge and Huddersfield. The Manchester and Leeds main line through Cooper Bridge had been opened seven years earlier since when passengers for Huddersfield had to undertake the final part of their journey by horse-drawn bus.

It would appear that for many years prior to the opening of the railway to Huddersfield there were various proposals put forward and, as time passed, increasing demands for connection to a growing national network. The first proposal came shortly after the opening of the Stockton and Darlington Railway in 1825 when there was a suggestion from Manchester businessmen for a railway between Manchester and Leeds which would have followed the route of the existing canal through Huddersfield. Nothing, however, came of this. Ultimately though Manchester and Leeds were connected in 1840 by a company of the same name, subsequently to become the Lancashire and Yorkshire Railway Company, the nearest station to Huddersfield on this line being Cooper Bridge, some 4½ miles from the town. Passengers for Huddersfield were conveyed from Cooper Bridge to the White Swan Inn by Elam's horse buses.

Regular travellers became impatient with this arrangement and in 1842 the Manchester and Leeds Company was pressurised to build a branch line into the town. As a consequence the company arranged a survey of the valley between Cooper Bridge and Huddersfield, followed by a meeting with the petitioners. The meeting was reported as being 'very strong' as the survey followed the lowest part of the valley whereas the petitioners wanted a line at a higher level which would provide the better option of a subsequent extension into Lancashire. The meeting eventually collapsed in disarray when a company spokesman expressed the view that 'Huddersfield is not worth stopping a train for'.

With the demise of this proposal a local company was formed with the express intention of constructing the line along the higher point in the valley and later joining up with the Sheffield, Ashton-under-Lyne and Manchester Railway at Stalybridge. This company was formed on 1st December, 1844, with the support of the canal company, and was named the Huddersfield and Manchester Railway and Canal Company. The first Board of Directors of the company was - William Aldam (Chairman), Joseph Armitage, William Bailey, William Leigh Brook, Francis Carbut, Thomas Firth, George Calvert Holland, James Lees, Cornelius Randell and Joseph Walker.

The Act authorising construction of the railway was passed on 26th April, 1845. According to the report which appeared in the *Leeds Mercury* on 3rd May, 1845 (at the time Huddersfield did not have its own local newspaper),this became a day of great rejoicing.

Bells were 'instantly set in motion and the whole population rose from their slumbers, and music paraded the town'. Mutual congratulations and rejoicings spread to the villages around the town, and it was declared 'Huddersfield has

Joseph Kaye (1780-1858), builder of Huddersfield railway station and many other buildings in the town, including the adjacent George Hotel. He was a local builder of some repute, and in addition to being a builder he was a stone merchant, quarry owner, lime burner, mill owner, malter and brewer. The photograph is taken from an anonymous oil painting of about 1825 now in Huddersfield Art Gallery.

Kirklees Metropolitan Council, Huddersfield Art Gallery

arisen and posterity will remember this period with proud delight'.

William Leigh Brook, a Director of the company, cut the first sod on the Huddersfield - Cooper Bridge section at Deighton on 10th October, 1845 and the line was to take approximately two years to construct at an estimated cost of £63,000.

In addition to the line itself Huddersfield station was to be a building of great significance.

A largely open site was chosen for the station known locally as 'Tumbling Fields' due to its previous use by clowns and jugglers. A primitive Methodist Chapel occupied a part of the site and had to be demolished, the final service being held on 17th May, 1846. The company provided a replacement chapel in the nearby Northumberland Street. Architecturally the station was to be one of the finest in the country. The architect was James Pigot Pritchett (1789-1868) who practised in London until 1813, after which he moved to York. He also designed Huddersfield Parish Church. The builder was Joseph Kaye (1780-1858), a local builder of some repute who also built the George Hotel, which is adjacent to the station, plus many other buildings in the town. In addition to being a builder Kaye was a stone merchant, quarry owner, lime burner, mill owner, malter and brewer. The building was described by Ian Nairn as a 'kind of stately home with trains in'.

The foundation stone is reputed to have weighed almost 6 tons and was laid on 9th October, 1846 by Earl Fitzwilliam, who was Lord Lieutenant and brother-in-law to the Ramsdens. It was clearly another day of great rejoicing and was declared a public holiday.

The *Leeds Mercury* was still the source of local news at this time and the edition of 10th October, 1846 carried an account of the laying of the foundation stone.

According to the report, which carried the headline 'Great Rejoicing at Huddersfield Yesterday', a general public holiday was declared and it would appear that the majority of the town's population joined in the celebrations. This has become a difficult concept to imagine as new services/facilities in the late 20th century rarely capture the imagination of even a small percentage of the population.

The foundation stone was laid by the Right Honourable Earl Fitzwilliam. The day began with the ringing of the parish church bells and the official ceremony was preceded by a procession of civic dignitaries and local VIPs. For those who know the town the procession followed the route: Kirkgate, Cross Church Street, Queen's Street, Ramsden Street, New Street, Westgate and then on to the site of the station. The procession was lead by a band and included the Chief Constable (on horseback), police, contractors, freemasons, magistrates, clergy, architect, engineers, MP for the Borough (W.R.C. Stansfield), Directors etc.

A large crowd gathered at the station site to greet the procession, which arrived in a shower of rain. The section of the building selected for the foundation stone laying was the centre wing and prior to laying the stone Earl Fitzwilliam placed what would now be called a 'time-capsule' in a recess. The actual vessel was a bottle and it contained the previous Saturday's *Leeds Mercury* and examples of all the different coins in use at that time. After insertion the recess was filled with concrete and topped with a brass plaque bearing the following inscription:

Huddersfield railway station *c.* 1908. Designed by J.P. Pritchett and built by Joseph Kaye in 1845/6 at a cost of £20,000, it has been described as 'a kind of stately home with trains in'.
Author's Collection

The George Hotel, Huddersfield. The hotel is in St George's Square, adjacent to the railway station, and was built by Joseph Kaye, the builder of the station. It was at a meeting in this hotel that Rugby League football was born. *Author*

The foundation stone of the Huddersfield station of the Huddersfield and Manchester Railway and Canal Company, built under the direction of the Board of Directors, was laid by Rt Hon. Earl Fitzwilliam, this 9th day of October AD 1846, in the tenth year of the reign of Her Majesty Queen Victoria; J.B. Pritchet & Son, Architects; Joseph Kaye, Builder.

Directors
William Aldam Junior Esq. MP Frickley Hall, Doncaster, Chairman
Joseph Brook, Esq., Greenhead, Huddersfield, Deputy Chairman
George Armitage, Egerton, Huddersfield
Thomas France Bennett, Liverpool
William Leigh Brook, Meltham Hall, Huddersfield
William Bayley, Stamford Lodge, Stalybridge
Thomas Firth, Toothill, Huddersfield
George Loch Pexhill, Warrington
Joseph Starkey, Woodhouse, Huddersfield
Jas Lees, Delph, Saddleworth
Joseph Stocks, Shibden Hall, Halifax
Thomas Varley, Egerton, Huddersfield
William Gilmour, Secretary: Alfred S. Gee, Engineer

Immediately afterwards the foundation stone was laid, it being lowered into place under the direction of the contractor, Joseph Kaye. Earl Fitzwilliam then said the following few words,

Well, gentlemen, having performed the last act in the ceremony of laying this stone, I can only say that I hope the work of which it is the beginning will realise the anticipations of those who originated it, and that it will be as permanent a source of prosperity to the town and neighbourhood, as the solidity of the structure about to be raised upon it.

In conclusion freemasons of the province scattered on the stone a quantity of corn, wine and oil, being the emblems of plenty, cheerfulness and joy. The procession then re-formed in the same order as previously, taking Directors and invited guests to the George Hotel for the inevitable meal which would serve to conclude the ceremony.

Around 360 people attended the dinner and according to the report the room at the George Hotel was 'tastefully decorated with evergreens and choice flowers, which hung in festoons around the room'. The Chairman of the Huddersfield and Manchester Railway and Canal Co., William Aldam, proposed a toast to Earl Fitzwilliam who responded saying it had given him great pleasure to assist in laying the foundation stone of a structure from which the town and its inhabitants would derive great personal accommodation, and from which commerce would derive great means of extension. On some points indeed it was still a problem what effect the great railway communication would have upon the community, and upon the particular districts which were immediately intersected by these lines. That the general tendency would be to the general good he entertained no doubt, but in respect to particular effects upon particular localities he ventured to think that the problem was not yet solved. It could and must go forward notwithstanding the opposition of parties who, they might depend upon it, would now begin to be opponents. He ventured that nevertheless the extension of railways would go on until the whole country was saturated with railway communication, this period being coincidental with the period at which the profit on capital invested in railways would be no greater than upon any other species of investment. He believed that period would come but until it arrived railways would be extended, despite the opposition from those who, whatever their motives, might think it better that the railway system should stop now.

After these thought-provoking words which seem to bear an uncanny resemblance to modern motorway development, the Earl made reference to the station building itself, commenting that he hoped the beauty of the fabric would rival the architecture of the model displayed before them and that the solidity and mass of the great stone he had had the satisfaction of hammering into place would be the solid prosperity of Huddersfield and of the extension of its commercial intercourse. A number of toasts followed after which the silver trowel used in the laying of the foundation stone was presented to the Earl. It bore the following inscription:

> Presented by the Directors of the Huddersfield and Manchester Railway and Canal Company to the Rt Hon. Earl Fitzwilliam on the occasion of his laying the first stone of the Huddersfield station on Friday 9th October, 1846.
> William Aldam Junior MP, Chairman
> Joseph Brook, Deputy Chairman
> Pritchett and Son, Architects.

As a gesture to those who were to build the station the Directors entertained to dinner in the afternoon some 170 employees of Joseph Kaye, these being masons, delvers and joiners.

The station was built at the joint expense of the Huddersfield and Manchester Railway and Canal Company and the Manchester and Leeds Railway Co. (later to become the Lancashire and Yorkshire Railway Co.).

Construction of the railway and the station proceeded and some 22 months after cutting the first sod at Deighton, and 10 months after the official laying of the foundation stone to Huddersfield station, the railway line into Huddersfield was completed, and the official opening took place on Monday 2nd August, 1847. Yet again the events of this momentus and vitally important day in the life of Huddersfield were described in the *Leeds Mercury* on 7th August, 1847.

Once more an important stage in the development of the railway into and through Huddersfield gave rise to a day of great rejoicing for most of the people of the town. The official opening of the stretch between Huddersfield and Cooper Bridge took place on a Monday following shortly after a Borough election. By the accounts it would appear that local elections aroused much more interest at that time than they do now. The article in the *Leeds Mercury* was at great pains to point out the difficulties that passengers from Huddersfield had experienced since the opening of the Manchester and Leeds Railway in 1833 when they had had to join trains at Brighouse or Cooper Bridge after travelling from Huddersfield by omnibus, the service having 'frequently been vexatious and trying both to the public and travellers'.

As with the earlier celebrations for the laying of the Huddersfield station foundation stone the ringing of the Parish Church bells played an important part in the day. The first official train was to run from Huddersfield to Cooper Bridge and in anticipation of large crowds arrangements had been made at Huddersfield to protect people from the potential dangers of the railway by providing barriers and many policemen. A triumphal arch was erected over the railway, circled in evergreens and flowers. Tricoloured flags were placed on each pedestal. The flags had a blue middle, white borders and red corners each formed in squares to show that the works of the railway had been constructed in squareness and solidity. Union Jacks were erected on sections of the station and on poles in the station yard together with red and white streamers bearing the insignia 'Huddersfield and Manchester Railway'.

Prior to the opening the line and works had been inspected by Captain Simmons, the Government Inspector of Railways, and it was reported that he had 'pronounced a very favourable opinion of the works, not merely in regard to their stability, but also for the beauty of workmanship and quality of materials'.

In terms of railway construction in the hilly West Riding of Yorkshire this stretch of line had not proved to be a particularly difficult task. The most notable work was, and remains to this day, a viaduct which was traversed immediately on leaving Huddersfield. The *Leeds Mercury* described it as 'one of the noblest structures of the kind in England'.

For the technically minded the viaduct consists of 43 square and four oblique arches. A skew arch over the Bradford Road is constructed at an angle of 37 degrees 30 minutes and 30 ft from the road to the railway track, with a versed sine of 9 ft 6 in. and a chord line of 67 ft. A model of this bridge was on display in the dining room of the George Hotel plus a geometrical drawing measuring 4 ft 6 in. by 2 ft 6 in., which had been prepared by Mr Josephus J. Roebuck, contractor's assistant. Mr Roebuck was responsible for designing and supervising the construction of all the oblique bridges for the full extent of the contract.

The first train left Huddersfield at ten minutes before 12 o'clock mid-day and travelled the 3¾ miles to Cooper Bridge in ten minutes. The train consisted of about 12 carriages and was pulled by two locomotives. The carriages were filled in the first instance by Directors, shareholders and their families, the remainder being filled with local inhabitants. It would appear that the latter were on a 'first come, first served' basis as it is recorded that the journey was free of charge. At the rear of the train were two open carriages occupied by military bands and the leading locomotive was driven by Mr Roche, the Manager of the locomotive department.

On arriving at Cooper Bridge Junction Joseph Brook, Vice-Chairman to the company, named the two engines *Aldam* and *Huddersfield* by smashing a bottle of champagne over them. Captain Binstead of the Manchester and Leeds Railway Company was also present during this ceremony. Mr Brook spoke to those present saying he hoped the opening of the line today would be an auspicious event in benefiting the town and commerce of Huddersfield. He congratulated the engineers and contractors on the manner in which the work had been executed so far, and remarked that they had given perfect satisfaction to Captain Simmons, the inspector; indeed that gentleman had remarked that he had rarely seen railway works so solidly and efficiently put together.

The train then returned to Huddersfield to be greeted with cheers and a band playing the National Anthem. Then, at approximately 2.0 pm, 600 workmen were served with dinner on temporary tables erected close to the station. The Directors and engineers dined at the George Hotel but it is recorded that 'the business transacted was of a strictly private nature'.

In conclusion the article noted two further points:

1. When open throughout, and together with the Leeds/Dewsbury line currently under construction, there will be a saving of 20 miles in the railway journey between Manchester and Leeds.
2. Goods traffic would continue to be conveyed by waggon to and from Brighouse railway station for the foreseeable future.

By the time this line was officially opened the Huddersfield and Manchester Railway and Canal Co. had been absorbed into the London & North Western Railway Co. This latter company was originally formed in 1846 by the amalgamation of the Liverpool and Manchester, London and Birmingham and the Grand Junction Railways. Several smaller companies were also involved, including the Huddersfield and Manchester. The Act incorporating the LNWR was dated 9th July, 1847. As a point of interest the Huddersfield and Manchester had previously approached the Lancashire & Yorkshire Railway Co. with a view to incorporation, but had been rejected.

One of the engines which pulled the first train was named *Aldam* after William Aldam MA, Chairman of the Huddersfield and Manchester Co. The locomotive had a 2-2-2 wheel arrangement and was built by Sharp, Roberts and Co. of Manchester. In August 1849 it was numbered 444 by the LNWR and in 1862 it was rebuilt as a saddle tank. It was scrapped in 1873.

It is interesting to note from the article that passengers were also conveyed by coach to and from Brighouse station in addition to Cooper Bridge.

Huddersfield station was not to be completed until 1850, three years after the opening of the railway. In the early days the station consisted of a single long platform and there were separate booking offices at each end for the Lancashire & Yorkshire and London & North Western Railway companies with dining rooms in the centre. The armorial bearings of the Lancashire & Yorkshire and Huddersfield and Manchester Companies were located over the respective booking offices, where they can be seen to this day. The companies each had their own goods stations.

The station facade is 416 feet long. It is an imposing building which is largely unchanged from the original. Norman Culley writes of the architectural style as below:

The main portico may be defined as being 'hexa-style' (i.e. 6-domed) and of the Corinthian Order. The Order is a slight variant of that of the portico of the Pantheon, Rome. The two porticos at the ends of the facade may be defined as 'tetra-style' (i.e. 4-columned) and are also of the Corinthian Order, being probably a slight variant of the Order of the Temple of Vesta of Tivoli. The connecting colonnades are of the same Order similar to the end porticos.

Chapter Three

Legislative Background to the Line

The Act authorising construction of the branch line from Huddersfield to Kirkburton was passed by Parliament on 28th July, 1863, 16 years after the railway first came to Huddersfield.

Various proposals were put forward before this and since which were aimed at developing a through route from Huddersfield to Barnsley and the Yorkshire coalfield. It is interesting to look at how the development went by considering these options.

The first mention of a railway into the parish of Kirkburton was in 1845 when the Huddersfield and Sheffield Junction Railway Act included a power to build a branch railway 'terminating at a Town or place called Holmfirth in the Parish of Kirkburton'. This was followed in 1846 by the surveying of a possible route through Clayton West and the Kirkburton Valley by Joseph Locke. He was an associate of George Stephenson and is remembered today by Locke Park at Barnsley. Whilst the former proposal did materialise the latter came to nothing.

The year 1852 saw the next proposal embodied in a local scheme titled 'West Riding Direct and Junction Railway'. This scheme, which was also not to materialise, included the following, 'to provide railway traction of a local nature between Huddersfield and Dalton, Kirkheaton, Fenay Bridge and Kirkburton, Shelley, Skelmanthorpe and Clayton West'.

In 1862 the Midland Railway Company showed an interest in a route from Barnsley to Huddersfield through Clayton West and Kirkburton. Towards the end of 1862 the Kirkburton Local Board Minute Book for the 11th December carried the following entry, 'Moved that the consent of the Local Board be given to a proposition for a railway from Huddersfield to Kirkburton'. This was carried unanimously but members were concerned that local rights should not be destroyed by the railway.

And so it was on 28th July, 1863 that the London & North Western Railway Co. obtained Parliamentary powers to build the branch from Huddersfield to Kirkburton. After all the rejoicings and celebrations which accompanied the opening of the railway to Huddersfield and the building of the Huddersfield railway station, the obtaining of Parliamentary powers to build this branch appears to have passed almost unnoticed by the local community. There was local pressure to extend the line a further five miles beyond Kirkburton to Clayton West, but the LNWR thought there was insufficient traffic potential.

In spite of the powers to build the branch having been obtained a variety of additional proposals continued to arise which would have served to convert the branch into a through route. According to an undated *Parkin's Almanac*, on 4th April, 1864 a Bill was put before the Court of Referees for the Midland Railway to construct an extension from Barnsley to a junction with the LNWR at Kirkburton. About this time the Trade Directories first record a new public house in the village called the Railway Junction Inn. It is possible that it was given this name in anticipation of the proposed Barnsley junction, although for some time the area had been known locally as 'the Junction'. In the 1930s the public house was renamed 'The Three Owls', the name it still retains.

Further investigation of this latter project indicates that the Midland Railway would have had running powers into Huddersfield over the LNWR branch and that the two companies were to subsequently construct a joint extension to Halifax. The scheme was, however, withdrawn when the Lancashire & Yorkshire Railway Co. offered running powers to the Midland via Penistone. The extension was again put forward jointly in 1866 and 1867 and then finally withdrawn. A final point on this proposal. In April 1865, when agreement was reached between the LNWR and Midland on joint running powers, the LNWR also agreed to abandon its proposed terminus and put the money saved into a joint station between the two.

In recognition of a point made earlier by the Kirkburton Local Board, the Huddersfield Waterworks and Improvement Act 1876 included a clause for the protection of the Kirkburton branch where water mains crossed it.

Even after the construction and opening of the branch proposals continued which would have served to change its status. In 1882 a Hull, Barnsley and West Riding Junction Railway came under consideration. This would have involved a spur to form a junction with the Kirkburton branch at Fenay Bridge. Once again, the scheme failed to materialise. Then in 1894 a further plan was put forward by E. Brington-Barnes. This was named the Huddersfield and Midland North West Central Railway and would have involved a line between Sheffield and Cononley, near Skipton.

Finally, in 1895, the Midland again proposed a line from Barnsley to Huddersfield, which would have passed through Skelmanthorpe and Kirkburton. It was intended that it would continue through Brighouse and Bradford to join the existing Midland line at Bingley. This proposal was subsequently withdrawn in favour of a proposed line from Middlestown, near Wakefield to go via Thornhill Edge to Houses Hill and then on to Kirkheaton. This scheme also failed to materialise. Eventually the Midland Railway did proceed with a very much reduced scheme in 1898 between Huddersfield and Mirfield, which had no effect on the Kirkburton branch, and this was only to survive until 1937.

After all the proposals to join Huddersfield and Barnsley by a direct rail route such a service was finally provided in 1983 when the Huddersfield to Sheffield service was diverted between Penistone and Sheffield to a route through Barnsley.

Chapter Four

Construction

The first sod of the Kirkburton branch was cut at Deighton, near the junction with the main line, on 10th March, 1865. This was almost two years after the Parliamentary powers had been obtained and construction was to last for a period of 2 years 7 months.

Construction commenced with the laying of a contractor's siding at the branch junction. The contractor appointed was Eckersley and Bayliss. They in turn appointed as sub-contractors Messrs Sigley, Miles and Haynes for the viaducts and Messrs Fawcett & Son for the buildings.

Work on the line was very heavy and, according to reports, was witnessed with interest by inhabitants of Kirkburton. The works included two viaducts and 21 bridges. The first viaduct appeared shortly after leaving the junction at Deighton and was known as the Whitacre Mill viaduct. It was built on a curve with a radius of 22 chains to the mile. It has seven arches, each having a 94 ft span and a rise of 21 ft 4 in. The second viaduct, at Rowley, located between Fenay Bridge and Kirkburton stations, has six arches, each arch with a span of 42 ft and a rise of 21 ft. The bridges varied in shape and size with the largest and most spectacular crossing Wakefield Road with a single span of 94 ft. This bridge, which no longer exists, was located between Kirkheaton and Fenay Bridge stations.

The line was initially constructed as single track throughout although sufficient land was taken to allow for a double track, which was presumably the intention had it been extended to form a through route to Barnsley. In addition a large area of land was taken between Kirkheaton station and the bridge over Wakefield Road for the construction of an extensive goods yard had the line been extended.

Although the works were said to be heavy there were no tunnels on the line. There were though two very deep cuttings in the vicinity of Fenay Bridge station which required the removal of half a million cubic yards of earth. Much of this was used in the building of embankments on the line. In addition the works at the Kirkburton station site were very heavy involving the construction of extensive retaining walls, the largest being some 28 ft high.

It would appear that for almost 12 months the construction works progressed largely according to plan and that the works were understood to be well forward. In particular the viaducts at Deighton and Rowley were in an 'advanced position'. Then on 15th February, 1866 a major set back occurred with the collapse of two arches of the Whitacre Mill viaduct at Deighton. There was an obvious intention, however, that this set back, which was to cost between £1,000 and £1,200, would not jeopardise the completion date of the work.

The incident, which was no doubt a major news item at the time, was extensively reported in what was by now Huddersfield's own newspaper, the *Huddersfield Examiner*. The paper was published weekly and the incident report appeared in the issue of 17th February, 1866. The following details are taken from that report. The fall occurred early on the Thursday morning. A detailed description of the viaduct, which was noted as being about 200 yds from the Leeds and Huddersfield Turnpike road, revealed that:

. . . it consists of seven arches, each 64 ft span, with a rise of 21 ft 4 in. from the springers, which are of stone of 3 ft 6 in. through the centre, and each arch is 8 ft 4 in. thick. The abutments are 10 ft thick, and the piers 8 ft 6 in. thick, and 28 ft long, but were somewhat narrower at one end than the other, because the viaduct is built on a curve with a radius of 22 chains. Most of the piers are upwards of 12 ft above the surface, and they all stand on foundations sunk several feet deep, and are 12 ft wide and 32 ft long, or thereabouts. The length of the viaduct is about 150 ft, and in its course it crosses the canal, the mill goit, and the River Colne, the goit of the river running under the fourth and fifth arches, and the canal under the first arch.

At the time of the accident the first and second arches had been completed up to the strong course, and the centres had been removed some two months earlier, whilst the other arches were at different stages of construction with the third and fourth most advanced.

Messrs Sigley, Miles and Haynes, were the builders of the viaduct with the work being overseen by the main contractors, Messrs Eckersley and Bayliss. The inspector was Mr Drinkwater who was assisted by his manager, Mr Godfrey. Pressed red brick manufactured at Brighouse was used for the main construction and it was faced with fire bricks manufactured at the works of Mr E. Brooke of Fieldhouse, a site alongside and connected to the main line railway. Interestingly the mortar used was ground in a machine designed for this purpose and driven by a small steam engine.

After the centres had been removed from the two first arches a small subsidence or depression had been noticed in the second arch of about two inches, two thirds of the distance between the springers and the centre of the arch. This was not expected to lead to the arch falling, but it was intended to re-build this part of the work. Prior to the accident the weather had been wet before turning to frost.

The collapse of the viaduct occurred at about two o'clock on Tuesday morning with a crash that could be heard apparently for some distance. Police Constables Wrigglesworth and Currie, patrolling several hundred yards away at the bottom of Deighton heard the noise and believed that the boiler had burst at Whitacre mill. Wrigglesworth ran towards the noise to find that one of the arches had fallen and he called up Mr Miles, the contractor's representative living nearby. He went to the site to find several others already there, to see that the second arch when falling had dragged down and caused the first arch to fall, with the debris completely blocking the canal and preventing the passage of any boats. The bricks of the first arch formed an embankment which rose several feet above the water of the canal, but fortunately the water could flow through the opening in this embankment, and there was no flooding beyond that caused by the wave raised by the sudden fall of so many tons of brickwork into the canal, which at that point is considerably higher than the field alongside which it passes. The brickwork of the second arch lay in a heap largely between the pier which had supported it, and assisted the second pier to withstand the pressure of the third arch, a pressure probably of many tons. Immediate steps were taken to remove the bricks out of the canal with men being sent for from as far afield as Saddleworth and other places by Mr Greenwood, the canal superintendent.

More than 60 men were employed to clean the canal which was completed by the Thursday night. The second pier had apparently not been damaged by the fall but it was strengthened to enable it to withstand the pressure in the form of large beams of timber placed against it. Every precaution was taken to prevent any further fall. The fall of the arches appeared to have been caused by the too early removal of the centres. The rebuilding was to take some months, but overall it was not expected to delay the opening of the line as there remained lots of work to do. At this time work on the viaduct at Rowley, Kirkburton, was well advanced.

As construction continued a number of references to the work were recorded in the Minute books of the Kirkburton Local Board, these being:

1st June, 1866: Deputation to be appointed respecting the footpath in the plantation on the Dean Side - site of the station. (Excavation work for the railway had cut through a footpath which provided a link between Highburton and North Road.)

7th February, 1867: Ordered that the Clerk make a complaint to the Engineer of the LNWR Co. respecting the bad state of the road at Far Dean. (From this reference it is assumed the road was damaged when building the railway bridge across the road.)

5th September, 1867: Ordered that the Clerk write to the Secretary of the LNWR Co. to make a footpath from Highburton to Dean Bottom without further delay. (The ultimate effect from this reference was the construction of a footbridge over the line just to the Fenay Bridge side of Kirkburton station. This footbridge features on many photographs, including one of the first train arriving at Kirkburton.)

After the unfortunate accident with the Whitacre Mill viaduct work appears to have progressed on the line in a satisfactory way. The line itself was completed by February 1867 but the opening had to be delayed for seven more months to allow construction of the stations and due to difficulties in excavating the station site at Kirkburton. Although the total construction period was less than three years the local inhabitants are reported as being relieved when the promised opening date of 7th October, 1867 was adhered to as apparently more than one earlier date had been suggested but not adhered to.

The goods facilities were not, however, completed at the time of the opening for passengers which meant a further delay before facilities could be offered for the handling of goods.

Whitacre Mill viaduct crossing the Huddersfield canal. It was at this point, on 15th February, 1866, that two arches of the viaduct collapsed whilst still under construction.

Author

The first passenger train to reach Kirkburton, LNWR in 1867. The locomotive is a 2-4-0 tank with 5 ft wheels of F. Trevithick's design, some of which were conversions of Allan type 2-4-0 goods locomotives. The first of these tanks went into service in 1856 and there were ultimately more than 100 of them at work.

Chapter Five

Official Opening

The line opened officially on Monday 7th October, 1867, the first train leaving Huddersfield at 7.00 am. It was a wet day but in spite of the conditions there was a good turn out and it would appear that everyone was in good spirits. Unlike many other railway openings, and in particular the events which marked the laying of the foundation stone to Huddersfield station and the opening of the railway into Huddersfield, the LNWR decided to open this particular branch without any form of ceremony. Local people were not put off by this, however, and the contractors, Eckersley and Bayliss, laid on an official celebration.

Prior to the official opening the railway had been inspected by Lt Col Hutchinson RE on behalf of the Lords of the Committee of Privy Council for Trade. On 5th September, 1867 the LNWR wrote to the Board of Trade indicating its intention to open the branch on 16th September and that the works would be completed and ready for inspection on 9th September. Lt Col Hutchinson was appointed as the inspecting officer and the initial inspection took place on 14th September, 1867 after which Lt Col Hutchinson advised the Secretary of the Railway Department at the Board of Trade 'that the branch line to Kirkburton cannot be opened to passenger traffic without danger to the public using the same'. The reasons for this conclusion, as detailed in Lt Col Hutchinson's letter, were:

1. Problems with the signalling arrangements at the junction of the branch with the main line.
2. Work required completing on some of the iron bridges.
3. There was some work to complete on the Whitacre Mill viaduct.
4. Inadequate locking arrangement for the points on the double track sections at the junction with the main line and at Kirkheaton and Kirkburton.
5. Sinking of a bridge abutment (at 3.77 miles) and a culvert arch (at 3.76 miles).
6. Work to complete on the viaduct near Kirkburton.
7. Rearrangement of certain goods sidings at Kirkburton.
8. Chock hocks required at the Kirkheaton sidings.

As a consequence of this letter, Thomas Gray of the Railway Department of the Board of Trade wrote to the Secretary of the LNWR on 16th September, 1867 indicating the Lords of the Privy Council for Trade were to postpone the opening of the line to passengers for a period of one calendar month.

The inspecting officer's report must have stirred the company into action though as a follow up inspection took place on 27th September, 1867, when Lt Col Hutchinson was able to report that 'the deficiencies noted in my report of the 14th inst. have been made good'. Nevertheless there remained a problem as this report went on to state 'No undertaking has been received as to the proposed method of working the line, but upon its receipt there would be no objection to their Lordships sanctioning the opening of this branch line'. This was followed on 28th September with a letter from the Board of Trade to the LNWR confirming that the line could open providing a satisfactory undertaking was received as to the proposed method of working of traffic. Finally on 2nd October the LNWR wrote to the Board of Trade acknowledging receipt of their letter of 28th September and enclosing an undertaking to work the Kirkburton branch on the Train Staff system only for so long as it remained a single line. Thus at long last the way was clear for the line to be opened.

By now Huddersfield had two local papers, the *Huddersfield Chronicle* and the *Huddersfield Examiner*. Both were published weekly and both of them carried an extensive account of the events of the opening day in the editions published on Saturday 12th October, 1867. The following accounts reflect the reports in both of these papers.

According to the reports the opening took place after many unavoidable disappointments. The departure of the first train for Kirkburton from Huddersfield was timed for seven o'clock on Monday morning, the locomotive pulling the train being decorated for the occasion. The articles referred to great difficulties being encountered in the construction of the line and went on to describe the line and the works involved. The branch itself was 4½ miles long, leaving the main Huddersfield/Leeds line at Whitacre Mill junction, about two miles from Huddersfield. The line crossed Leeds Road by means of a girder bridge, and continued over the canal and River Colne by a viaduct of seven arches, each of 64 ft span, and rising 24 ft 6 in. This viaduct was on a curve of 22 chains radius, which had a light and cheerful appearance as a consequence of the brick finish used. Several other bridges were passed before reaching the first station, which was at Kirkheaton. This had spacious overall accommodation in anticipation of large amounts of traffic. A neat little wooden station building had been erected which provided for the safety and convenience of passengers. The next notable bridge was that which passed over the Wakefield Road, near the Tandem Inn, which spanned a distance of 94½ ft. Further on a bridge was constructed near the home of a Mr Abraham Brierley and he had laid out the grounds attractively, improving the overall appearance at that point. The next place of note was recorded as the celebrated spa well, just prior to Fenay Bridge station, where a double bridge had been constructed, one arch crossing the road and the other the well. Immediately following this was Fenay Bridge, where again a neat station had been erected, opposite the mills of Messrs Riley Brothers. Approaching Kirkburton was the viaduct at Dogley, to the rear of Messrs Kenyon's premises, and over the mill goit and valley, consisting of six arches, each 42 ft span, and rising 21 ft. Half a mile further along the terminus of the branch was reached, having travelled through what was then, and still remains, a picturesque piece of landscape scenery. The obstacles facing the builders of the station at Kirkburton were substantial but the work had been completed to the satisfaction of the Government Inspector. The construction of huge retaining walls had proved expensive and there was an embankment some 28 ft high. The resultant site though was spacious to deal with the anticipated level of goods traffic. The number of bridges on the line (excluding viaducts) was 21, and the cutting for the various embankments was nearly 300,000 yards. At Kirkburton alone the extent of cutting was nearly 200,000 yards. As far as the main line works were concerned the original contracts had been completed the previous

February, the delay in opening the line being attributed to a subsequent contract for the stations, and the almost insuperable difficulties which were met with in excavating the site at Kirkburton together with the accident at the Whitacre Mill viaduct.

Among the passengers on the first train were: Mr Bayliss, one of the contractors; Mr W. Sutton, superintendent of the district; Mr Buck, resident engineer; Mr Thompson, station master at Huddersfield; Mr John Fawcett and others. The engine and carriages were decorated with flags, evergreens etc., and as the train began to move slowly from the station salutes were fired. In spite of the poor weather large crowds lined the route and cheers were raised at many locations as the train came into view. A brass band travelled to Huddersfield by one of the later trains, and remained in the town until night. The railway officials were entertained at the Station Hotel; a group of local Kirkburton inhabitants dined at the Spring Grove Inn and about 30 gentlemen who had been directly or indirectly connected with the opening of the line, were invited to a buffet at the George Hotel by Messrs Eckersley and Bayliss. The gentlemen who accepted these invitations were Messrs J. Freeman, J. Batley, George Crowther, G.H. Crowther, George Harper, George Moore, G. Mitchell Junior, J. Fawcett, H. Wigney, C. Riley, John Riley, Edward Riley, Joe Sheard, W. Sutton; H. Price, chemist and gas engineer of the LNWR Co., Crewe; J.W. Brown, CE, Engineer of the Meltham branch of the Lancashire & Yorkshire Railway Co.; G.B. Godfrey, CE, contractor's engineer; Inspector Normanton, J. Beaumont, goods superintendent and other gentlemen. After the meal the loyal toast was given by Mr Bayliss. Mr J. Freeman (Messrs Brook, Freeman and Batley, Solicitors to the company), proposed a toast to the company. He commented that the opening of the line was to him an interesting occasion, and no doubt to all present. A new line of communication had been opened up which would be most useful to the district. With regard to its future he could only hope that that which had been begun would be brought to a good end. It was he who proposed that the company should build the line, and, particularly as his advice had been taken, he hoped the undertaking would prove prosperous. The LNWR had served this district well, and the people were indebted to them for that. He hoped the line would be beneficial and fulfil all its aspirations. He further hoped the Kirkburton branch would meet with the support of the people, that the opening of the line would be the start of a new era in the district of Kirkburton. Mr W. Sutton, district superintendent, responded on behalf of the Directors, saying whilst it was a short line he hoped it would prove of great benefit to the district. It was the wish of the Directors that the district of Kirkburton should have every assistance with developing the traffic in this important woollen district. He did not believe they intended to end the line at Kirkburton and hoped that before long the Directors might issue an order to the contractor to go forward. He finished by saying he 'had never seen or travelled over a better finished line in the whole of his railway experience'.

Afterwards the 'health of the contractors' was responded to by Mr Bayliss who expressed his satisfaction with the way the various sub-contractors had carried out their work, and concurred with the idea that the Directors would eventually have to extend to Barnsley. Following a number of other toasts the proceedings were brought to a conclusion.

At Kirkburton and surrounding districts there was great rejoicing with parish church bells ringing, the Victoria Brass Band playing and flags flying throughout. In conclusion the *Huddersfield Chronicle* went on to quote one of their correspondents who was making a case for goods facilities at Fenay Bridge. The writer, who was one of many, was quoted as below:

> It is not my intention to reflect upon the judgement which has placed a goods station at Kirkheaton, and left Fenay Bridge without. Railway officials have, like other trades, their reasons for the step they take. A few facts may, however, lead to a reconsideration of the matter so far as Fenay Bridge and the district surrounding it is concerned, and these with your commission I will now give. Within a mile of Fenay Bridge station there are nearly 12 mills and manufacturers of different kinds, among them being Riley Brothers, J. & T. Kenyon, A. Brierley, Albert Midgley, Sam Midgley, Robert Scott, J.E. Taylor Brothers, Birks Mill, Sutcliffes Brewery, Midgleys Gas Works, Woodsome Corn Mill, Shaws Chemical Works, Jessops Chemical Works. The villages of Almondbury and Lepton are also within easy distance; the former which has a population of nearly 5,000 is less than a mile from Fenay Bridge, whilst it is two miles from Huddersfield. None of these firms can be expected to avail themselves of the station at Kirkheaton, seeing they would have to cart their goods long distances, along indifferent roads, and have to run the risk of delay in transmission incidental to roadside traffic. Rather than do this I feel they would prefer bringing them as heretofor to Huddersfield and sending them by either the North Western or any other company as they may feel disposed.

The locomotive which pulled the first train was a 2-4-0 tank, numbered 37. It was to a design by F. Trevithick and had 5 ft driving wheels. The first of these locomotives went into service in 1856, and ultimately there were more than 100 of them.

There are a number of other interesting points which can be gleaned from the articles. Worthy of mention is the garden of Mr Abraham Brierley, which appears to have been landscaped largely for the benefit of railway passengers, and the spa well adjacent to the station at Fenay Bridge. Also worthy of note is the information at the end of the article regarding manufacturing industry in the vicinity of Fenay Bridge station, a reminder that early railways were almost more important for the moving of raw materials and manufactured goods than for the travelling public. Additionally it seems clear from the comments made by Mr W. Sutton, district superintendent, that there was a clear expectation the line would be extended to Barnsley.

The articles referred to Kirkheaton as a 'pretty little station and at it full arrangements have been made for the carrying on of the goods and passenger traffic of the district'. In spite of this comment though the warehouses were not completed at the time of the official opening and the line was not to provide a service for goods traffic until the first day of 1868.

Finally on 10th September, 1932 the *Huddersfield Daily Examiner* carried an article detailing the recollections of a former Kirkburton man, 87 year-old Mr Hiram Hardcastle. In this the opening of the railway was referred to:

> He remembers too the branch railway from Huddersfield to Kirkburton being opened. There was great rejoicing on that occasion and on the first day it was opened the villagers were given as many free rides as they wanted.

Chapter Six

Operation

This chapter seeks to follow the operation of the branch from its official opening until 1930 when it was closed for regular passenger traffic. As mentioned earlier the goods warehouses were not completed at the time of the opening for passenger traffic. The delay was not too long, however, goods traffic commencing on New Year's Day, 1868. Furthermore there were only three passenger stations on the branch at this time, Deighton station not opening until Wednesday 30th August, 1871. The opening of the station was reported in what was by then the *Huddersfield Daily Examiner* of the same date, as below:

New Passenger Station at Deighton - This morning a new station was formally opened at Deighton on the Kirkburton branch of the London and North Western Railway and it will, no doubt, be a great boon to the people living in the village whose name the station bears. Yesterday Mr H.B. Corns, superintendent from Manchester, accompanied by Mr Thompson, station master at Huddersfield, went to Deighton and made the requisite arrangements for the opening. It has been arranged that all trains passing to and from Kirkburton shall stop at Deighton.

In the early days Deighton was a single platform station, as were the other three stations on the branch. Huddersfield station also consisted of one long platform at this time, and it was not until almost 20 years after the opening of the Kirkburton branch that further platforms were added. Additionally at the time of the opening the line passed through some beautiful countryside for the whole of its journey. So much so that an Isolation and Fever Hospital was built alongside the line and the Huddersfield Sanatorium was located at Mill Hill, not far from the line. Unfortunately, in many ways, this was not to last with the development of industry and other essential services to modern living, such as sewage works, particularly alongside the sections of the line nearest to Huddersfield. These in turn gave rise to a number of industrial connections which are described in the next chapter.

On 11th March, 1871 the *Huddersfield Examiner* carried an announcement that the landlord of the Rose and Crown Public House, Mr Lister Carter, intended to run a cab and dog cart from all the trains at Kirkburton then on to Shelley and to Clayton West. The article concluded:

. . . the need for something of this sort has been very much felt ever since the line was opened and Mr Carter will undoubtedly receive the encouragement and patronage which his public spirit so richly deserves.

The 10th August, 1872 saw an accident on the branch when an engine and portion of a train left the track immediately after leaving one of the stations. Unfortunately which of the stations it was is not recorded. The year 1882 was to see the commencement of work on widening the main line between

Huddersfield and Kirkburton Branch—(WEEK DAYS ONLY.)

	a.m.	a.m.	a.m.	a.m.	noon	p.m.	p.m.	p.m.	p.m.	p.m.
Huddersfield depart	6 55	8 5	10 25	...	12 40	4 55	6 6	...	...	...
Deighton	7 1	8 11	10 26	...	12 46	5 1	6 6	...	...	...
Kirkheaton	7 4	8 14	10 30	...	12 49	5 4	6 10	...	...	...
Fenay Bridge	7 9	8 19	10 34	...	12 53	5 9	6 14	...	...	...
Kirkburton arrive	7 13	8 23	10 38	...	12 58	5 13	6 18	...	...	...

	a.m.	a.m.	a.m.	a.m.	p.m.	p.m.	p.m.	p.m.	p.m.	p.m.
Kirkburton depart	5 50	7 20	8 30	10 45	...	2 5	5 55	6 55	7 35	8 45
Fenay Bridge	5 54	7 24	8 34	10 49	...	3 9	5 59	6 59	7 39	8 50
Kirkheaton	5 58	7 28	8 38	10 53	...	3 13	5 53	6 53	7 53	8 54
Deighton	6 13	7 32	8 42	10 57	...	3 17	5 57	6 57	7 57	8 58
Huddersfield arrive	6 13	7 40	8 50	11 4	...	3 21	5 47	6 7	7 42	9 30

A—Market Train, Saturdays only.

B—This Train leaves Huddersfield at 1.5 p.m. on Saturdays calling at intermediate Stations correspondingly later.

HUDDERSFIELD AND KIRKBURTON BRANCH.

WEEK DAYS.

	a.m.	a.m.	a.m.	a.m.	noon	p.m.	p.m.	p.m.	p.m.	p.m.	p.m.	p.m.
					B							**C**
HUDDERSFIELD depart	6 30	8 8	9 5	10 18	12 20	2 25	5 3	6 10	7 0	8 20	9 46	10 45
Deighton	6 36	8 14	9 11	10 24	12 26	2 31	5 9	6 16	7 6	8 26	9 51	10 51
Kirkheaton	6 40	8 18	9 15	10 28	12 30	2 36	5 13	6 19	7 10	8 30	9 55	10 55
Fenay Bridge	6 44	8 22	9 20	10 32	12 34	2 39	5 17	6 23	7 14	8 34	9 59	10 59
KIRKBURTON arrive	6 47	8 26	9 24	10 36	12 38	2 43	5 20	6 26	7 18	8 38	10 3	11 3

WEEK DAYS.

	a.m.	a.m.	a.m.	a.m.	a.m.	p.m.	p.m.	p.m.	p.m.	p.m.	p.m.	p.m.
							S		**S**		**T**	
KIRKBURTON depart	5 45	7 20	8 32	9 35	10 43	1 35	2 52	5 27	6 32	7 25	8 45	10 15	11 10
Fenay Bridge	5 50	7 25	8 37	9 40	10 47	1 40	2 57	5 31	6 36	7 30	8 50	10 18	11 15
Kirkheaton	5 54	7 29	8 41	9 44	10 51	1 44	3 1	5 35	6 40	7 34	8 54	10 24	11 19
Deighton	5 58	7 32	8 44	9 47	10 55	1 47	3 4	5 38	6 43	7 37	8 57	10 27	11 23
HUDDERSFIELD arrive	6 8	7 39	8 51	9 54	11 2	1 54	3 11	5 46	6 49	7 44	9 4	10 34	11 29

B—This Train leaves Huddersfield at 1.5 p.m. on Saturdays, calling at intermediate Stations correspondingly later.

C—Market Train, Tuesdays and Saturdays only.

S—Saturdays only.

T—Tuesdays only.

For list of Workmen's Tickets issued in this District, see page 144.

HUDDERSFIELD and KIRKBURTON.—London and North Western.

Down.

Miles		mrn	mrn	mrn	mrn	aft	aft	aft	aft	aft	aft	aft	aft	aft	aft	aft	aft
						Week Days only.				**Sats. only.**							
	Huddersfield dep.	6 30	7 50	9 10	10 20	12 25	1 30	2 27	4 25	5 20	...	6 12	7 8	59	10 29		
2	Deighton	6 36	7 56	9 16	10 26	12 31	1 36	2 33	4 31	5 26	...	6 18	7 5	9 5	10 35		
3	Kirkheaton	6 40	8 0	9 20	10 30	12 35	1 40	2 37	4 35	5 30	...	6 27	7 0	9 10	10 40		
4	Fenay Bridge & Lepton	6 44	8 4	9 24	10 34	12 39	1 44	2 41	4 39	5 35	...	6 26	7 14	9 13	10 44		
4½	Kirkburton arr.	6 48	8 8	9 28	10 38	12 43	1 48	2 45	4 54	5 40	...	6 30	7 18	9 17	10 48		

Up.

Miles		mrn	mrn	mrn	mrn	aft	aft	aft	aft	aft	aft	aft	aft	aft	aft
						Week Days only.						**Sats. only.**			
	Kirkburton dep.	6 12	7 15	8 15	9 33	10 42	12 50	1 40	2 0	...	5 48	6 35	7 23	9 22	
1	Fenay Bridge & Lepton	6 16	7 19	8 19	9 37	10 46	12 54	1 44	2 4	...	5 52	6 39	7 27	9 26	
2	Kirkheaton	6 20	7 23	8 23	9 41	10 51	12 58	1 48	2 8	...	5 56	6 43	7 31	9 30	
4	Deighton	489, 572, 574	6 24	7 27	8 27	9 45	10 57	1 2	1 52	2 12	...	6 0	6 47	7 34	9 34	
4½	Huddersfield 486 arr.	6 35	7 36	8 37	9 53	11 3	1 11	2 0	2 22	...	6 8	6 55	7 48	9 42	

Timetables for the Kirkburton branch: *top, April 1884; centre, November 1894; bottom, July 1922.*

Huddersfield and Bradley. The work, which took four years, allowed an increase in the number of lines from two to four. It was also the year when the Huddersfield Tramways became the first municipal system in the country to be operated by a corporation. The system was built to a gauge of 4 ft 7¾ in. to allow the running of standard gauge railway wagons. There is no record of this ever having taken place, however, although a coal delivery service was operated using two specially adapted trams.

In the early days of the branch there were nine trains each way Mondays to Fridays with one extra market train on Saturdays from Huddersfield to Kirkburton and two extra from Kirkburton to Huddersfield. Journey times from Huddersfield to Kirkburton averaged 18 minutes and 20 minutes in the reverse direction. All trains stopped at all the stations. There was never a Sunday service.

From time to time the Kirkburton Local Board considered items relating to the railway. On 15th May, 1884 concern was being expressed about the level of fares, as will be seen from the following extract from the Minute Book:

> That the clerk write to the L&NWR Co. requesting they reduce the price of the single third class railway fare between Kirkburton and Huddersfield which is now 6½ d. and to draw their attention to the distance by road.

Why the attention of the company was being drawn to the distance by road is not immediately clear but it became so when road transport started to provide meaningful competition.

In 1885 electric lighting was introduced on the trains. The LNWR had been one of the first to introduce gas lighting to the coaches when many other companies continued with oil lamps. Heating by footwarmers was, however, to remain until the turn of the century.

Passenger traffic was initially very good but 1890 saw the beginning of what was to be a steady decline. On 20th September of that year the steam tram service was extended to Waterloo which creamed off much of the potential traffic from Kirkheaton station. The distance by road was, and is, about three-quarters of the distance by train although train journey times were shorter. The trams were, though, much more convenient for large numbers of the local population.

By 1894 the number of trains had increased to 10 each way per day Mondays to Fridays with one additional train on Saturdays from Huddersfield to Kirkburton and two in the reverse direction. An extra attraction was a Tuesdays and Saturdays market train between Huddersfield and Kirkburton but a Tuesdays-only in the opposite direction.

On 1st September, 1897 Fenay Bridge station was renamed Fenay Bridge and Lepton, which was perhaps a more accurate reflection of its geographical location and the areas of population served. Throughout this time the Kirkburton Local Board continued to consider items connected with the railway and indeed were still concerned about the level of fares as will be seen from the following extract from the Minute books:

RAILWAY COLLISION AT HUDDERSFIELD. GOOD-FRIDAY, APRIL 21ˢᵗ 1905. (X.3.) COPYRIGHT.

Railway collision just outside Huddersfield station on Good Friday, 21st April, 1905. Huddersfield No. 2 signal box can be seen in the left background.
Author's Collection

Deputation to meet the railway company to urge the necessity of reducing the fare to 5*d*. single and 9*d*. for a return ticket by all trains except market trains, and that the market train arrangements be altered so as to convey passengers by all trains after one o'clock on Tuesdays, Fridays and Saturdays at the present fare of 8*d*. for the return journey.

It is interesting to note the virtual non-existence of inflation in those days.

An intriguing problem associated with the railway exercised the minds of the Local Board members on 5th January, 1899.

The clerk was asked to write to the L&NWR Co. drawing its attention to the complaints that had been received with reference to the nuisance arising from night soil being conveyed from Huddersfield to Kirkburton station and allowed to remain there until farmers from outlying townships carted it away. The clerk was to request that the traffic be either dispensed with or some means devised whereby it might be less obnoxious to the inhabitants and passengers.

Traffic on the line was to suffer a further decline with the electrification of the tram route between Huddersfield and Waterloo on 15th May, 1902. The year 1903 saw the installation of a connection from the branch to Elliott's brickworks which is described in more detail in the following chapter. In 1905 traffic was to be disrupted by probably the worst railway accident to occur in the Huddersfield district. It happened on Good Friday, 21st April,1905 at 2.30 pm when a collision took place involving a Lancashire & Yorkshire train and a London & North Western train just outside Huddersfield station blocking the line between the station and Kirkburton Junction. Two people died in the accident and 12 were injured.

As would be expected the accident was extensively reported in the local press and the following information is taken from the report which appeared in a special edition of the *Huddersfield Daily Examiner* which was published on the day after the accident.

The accident occurred at two-thirty in the afternoon close to the station but on the Kirkburton Junction side. Two trains were involved and it resulted in the deaths of two people, Ralph G. Farrand (23) of 6 Hall Royd Lane, Longwood and Catherine Yates Milne (46) of 54 Belgrave Street, Leeds. Many more were injured, the more serious being taken to Huddersfield Infirmary for treatment.

The trains which collided were a Lancashire & Yorkshire passenger train which left Bradford at 1.50 pm and an empty LNWR train of three carriages. The L&YR train was driven by W. Cliffe of Mirfield, the fireman being C. Lough. The LNWR train was driven by Fred Hague of Hillhouse, Huddersfield, with A. Nicholson as fireman.

The collision occurred on the viaduct just before entering the station. The L&YR train was approaching the station at a normal running speed when the driver saw the LNWR train on the same line, but by then it was too late to avoid a collision. The signals were in favour of the Bradford train, and against the LNWR train. The resultant collision was so violent that the tender of the LNWR engine was very badly damaged, as was the tender of the L&YR engine.

The L&YR train consisted of eight coaches, which included the guard's van whilst the first carriage had a parcels compartment. The force of the collision caused the carriage next to the tender to mount onto the next carriage, which was severely damaged. The roof of the second carriage and part of the carriage itself was forced onto the third carriage, but the rest of the train escaped without any damage and it remained on the track. The engine of the L&YR train was, however, knocked off the lines.

The interior of Huddersfield station *c.* 1910, looking from the island platform towards platform number 1. This view is looking towards Kirkburton Junction. *Kirklees Cultural Services*

The interior of Huddersfield station *c.* 1910, this time looking from number 1 platform towards the island platform. Huddersfield No. 1 signal box is on the left. This view is also looking towards Kirkburton Junction. *Kirklees Cultural Services*

At the time of the accident there were few people about as it was a holiday and some of the station staff were away. Those present though were immediately summoned to the scene of the disaster.

Dr W.G. Kilner Crosland, who lived nearby, heard the collision and was on the scene within a very short time. Similarly Mr H. Whiteley of the Huddersfield St John's Ambulance Brigade was on the station platform and was able to render immediate assistance. Other doctors who came to the scene included Doctors F.W. Robinson, J. Irvine, Porrits, Walker, F. Knaggs, Wright, Rolfe, Wilson, Horsfall, Edwards, Rawell and the House Surgeon at the Infirmary. Several of those rescued were able to get to the infirmary on their own. The rescue work though was very slow on account of the position of the carriages relative to one another.

The station master, Mr Joe Sykes, was on the scene shortly after the accident. At about 4 o'clock a railway crane was brought from Mirfield to assist in the work of clearing the line.

During the afternoon large crowds of people gathered on each side of the viaduct and barricades had to be erected to prevent them getting too near the railway as pieces from the wrecked coaches were falling over onto the road.

Those who lost their life in the accident were:

Ralph G. Farrand (23), of Blackburn Road, Birstall: Slater: fracture of the skull.

Catherine Yates Milne (46), of 56 Belgrave Street, Leeds: Widow: right leg crushed and other injuries.*

Those injured in the accident were:

Frances Shillito (28), married, 7 Barnsley Street, Nelson Road, Wyke: fracture of shoulder blade.

Emily Brearley (33), single, 8 Hall Road, Shipley: bleeding and other scalp wounds.

Joe Bamforth (32), Roundhill, Cleckheaton: shock and bruised ribs.

Frank Moore (27), Craven Lane, Gomersal: bruises and shock.

Arthur Nicholson (24), fireman, LNWR, Miriam Street, Fartown: bruises and shock.

The foregoing were taken to the Huddersfield Royal Infirmary.

J. Scott, commercial traveller, 11 Commercial Street, Huddersfield: shock and cut on the forehead.

E. Carter, Mark Bottom, Paddock: fingers lacerated.

George Western, St Peter's Street: shock and injury to the chest.

G. Brooke, Mirfield: cut and bruised.

Mrs Brook, Bingley: black eye.

W. Cliffe, driver, L&YR, Mirfield: scalded wrists.

C. Lough, fireman, L&YR, Mirfield: bruised left hip and cut on the left hand.

Later in 1905 the connection from the branch to Victoria Colliery was installed which is described in more detail in Chapter Seven.

On 3rd June, 1908 a new connection for public traffic was opened at the south end of Fenay Bridge station. The inspecting officer in this instance was Colonel Yorke. The connection was worked from a ground frame containing two levers locked by key on the electric train staff (which had been introduced in 1902). The object of the connection was to allow tailroping to be dispensed with.

At this time horses were used for carting goods from the railhead to the customer and it is worth noting that in 1908 four companies used the stables in viaduct street, near to Huddersfield station. These stables occupied the arches under the viaduct on the Kirkburton Junction side of the station. The four companies concerned were the LNWR, L&YR, Great Central Railway and Pickfords Ltd.

---

* Observant readers will notice that the addresses given here, for the passengers who lost their lives, differ from those given earlier. This anomaly occurred in the *Huddersfield Daily Examiner's* original report.

L & N.W.R. KIRKBURTON BRANCH — DEIGHTON.

New Up Platform & additional connections shewn by Red Colour.

Map showing new up platform to Deighton station on the Kirkburton branch, June 1916.

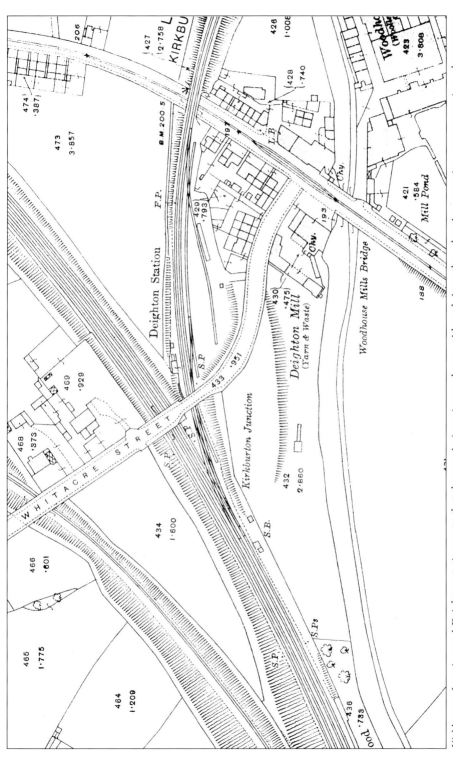

Kirkburton Junction and Deighton station; note that the up platform is not shown; although later than the plan opposite, not every minor change was recorded on the next issue of the OS map.

Reproduced from the 25", 1919 Ordnance Survey Map

Kirkburton Junction *c.* 1966, the train is travelling from Huddersfield towards Bradley. The Junction signal box can be seen on the left.   *F.J. Bullock*

Kirkburton Junction, 14th September 1969.   *F.J. Bullock*

Deighton station. The date is uncertain but the photograph was taken prior to 1916 at which time a second platform was added. *C. & K. Battye Collection*

An LNWR train shortly after leaving Kirkheaton, heading towards Deighton and Huddersfield. The 2-4-2T locomotive is pulling 6-wheel compartment coaches. *C. & K. Battye Collection*

STATION
KIRKHEATON

Kirkheaton station with a train from Huddersfield to Kirkburton pulled by an LNWR 2-4-2T. The photograph was taken prior to 1916, after which the service was provided by motor trains.

Lens of Sutton

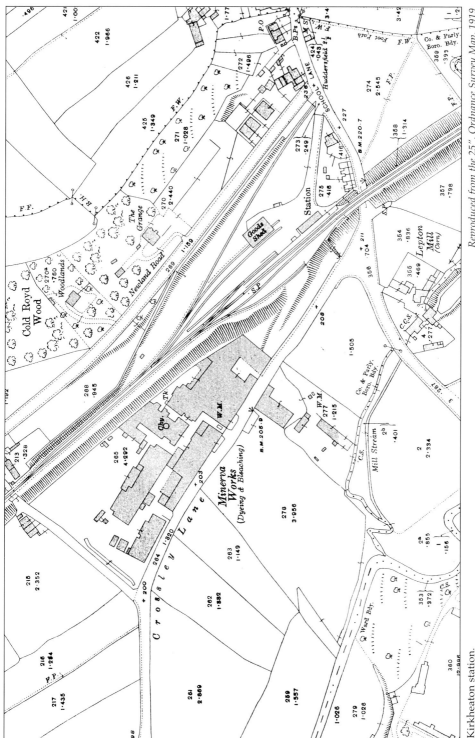

Reproduced from the 25", Ordnance Survey Map, 1919

Kirkheaton station.

WD 2-8-0 No. 90619 in Kirkheaton goods yard, 4th November, 1961.   *Geoff Lumb*

WD 2-8-0 No. 90619 passes through Kirkheaton station.   *Geoff Lumb*

The 1910 timetable on the branch showed a slight improvement over previous years with three additional trains. In 1911 the LNWR abolished second class accommodation, being the last of the English railway companies to do so.

The area around Fenay Bridge, Lepton and Gawthorpe boasted as many as six factories which, during World War I, produced explosives. Throughout the period of the War it is claimed that an average of four million hand-grenades were dispatched each year from Fenay Bridge station. The loading in the two-siding goods yard was undertaken by the station master and two female porters. It was also during World War I that British Dyes, later to become ICI, started producing chemicals at a site alongside the line and railway connection was provided direct from the branch in 1915. There was an unofficial Halt here for special trains carrying workers from Kirkburton. It was not used by workers from Huddersfield, however, as they used the trams.

As a consequence of the British Dyes development, improvement works were carried out at the junction of the branch with the main line, and an additional platform was added to Deighton station. These works are described in the following extract from a letter written by the LNWR to the Board of Trade on 6th June, 1916:

> In connection with some additional accommodation which has been provided for the British Dyes Ltd at Deighton Works, who are at present engaged on work for the Government, the company have provided a new platform on the up side of their Kirkburton branch at Deighton opposite the existing down platform and also two crossover lines between the up and down lines, the down line and siding connecting with the British Dyes Ltd works. I shall feel obliged if the Department will forward sanction to the new work, which is shown in red and pink on the enclosed plan, being brought into use when complete, pending inspection.

A further letter from the LNWR to the Board of Trade dated the 13th September, 1916 indicated that the new works were completed and could be inspected at anytime. The inspecting officer was Lt Col E. Druitt, and the following is his letter confirming the inspection:

Railway Department,
Board of Trade,
8 Richmond Terrace,
Whitehall,
London SW.
27th October, 1916

Sir,
I have the honour to report for the information of the Board of Trade that in compliance with instructions contained in your minute of 14th September, I have inspected the new works at Deighton on the Kirkburton branch of the LNWR.

At this place a new platform has been provided 300 ft long, 10 ft wide and 2 ft 9 in. above rail level with the usual overhang. It is approached by steps from an overbridge at the west end of the platform.

The new facing connections have been laid in, one laid from the down line to the British Dyes Ltd, and the other leading from the single line from Kirkburton to the up line.

The new connections and signals are worked from a new signal box containing 19

The interior of Kirkheaton goods shed, with the 25 cwt crane in the foreground.   *Geoff Lumb*

Kirkheaton yard and station: 20th March, 1963. The passenger station can be seen on the right of the picture, still apparently in good condition. *F.J. Bullock*

BR Standard class '4' 2-6-4T No. 80044 passes Tandem goods yard, near Kirkheaton with the Railway Enthusiasts Club special the 'Pennine Rose' on 2nd May, 1959. *Geoff Lumb*

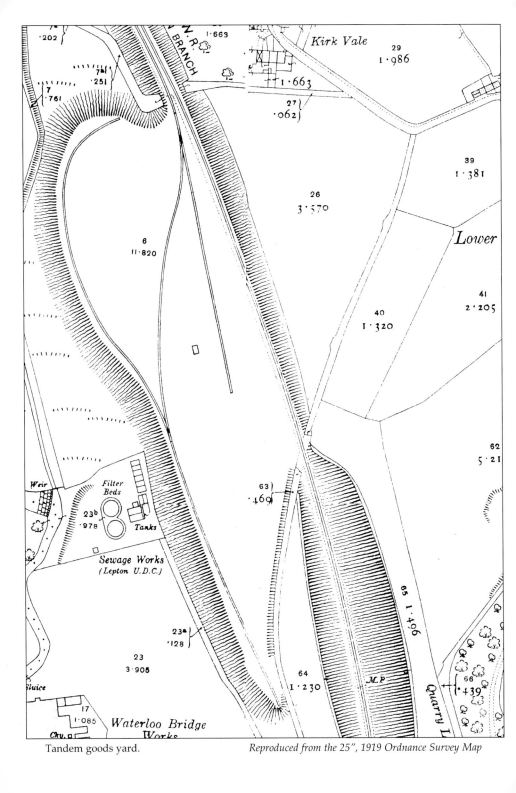

Tandem goods yard.

Reproduced from the 25", 1919 Ordnance Survey Map

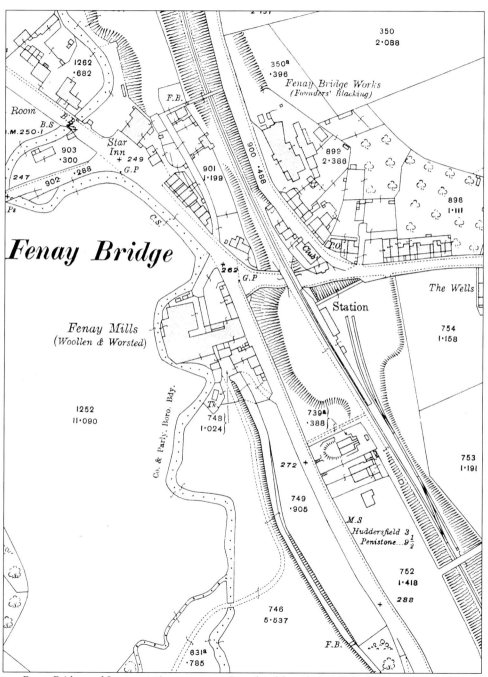

Fenay Bridge and Lepton station. *Reproduced from the 25", 1919 Ordnance Survey Map*

The 'Star Hotel', Fenay Bridge. The railway ran to the rear of these buildings and Fenay Bridge and Lepton station can be seen on the right-hand side, standing above the level of the buildings in the foreground.   *C. & K. Battye Collection*

A cruel enlargement of the previous photograph showing Fenay Bridge and Lepton station taken from Penistone Road and showing the junction with Station Road. The road surface at this time is still dirt.   *C. & K. Battye Collection*

working levers and 6 spares. The interlocking arrangements being satisfactory I can recommend the Board to sanction the use of the new works in question.
I have the honour to be, Sir
Your Obedient Servant,
E Druitt.

The year 1916 also saw the introduction of a motor train service. On 15th November of that year the *Huddersfield Daily Examiner* reproduced a poem from a Kirkburton resident who, according to the paper, had 'let himself go' on the novelties of the new motor train service, which was commonly known as 'Kirkburton Dick', to that village. This poem is quoted below:

If you're wanting a tip
For an afternoon trip
When you've got a few hours to spare
The motor express on the Kirkburton line
Reveals you a landscape exquisitely fine
And scenery rich and rare

With a puff and a slide
And a beautiful glide
The train leaves Huddersfield station
And the company you meet
Are a positive treat
For humour and gay conversation

Both Asquith and Law
With their wonderful 'jaw'
Are eclipsed by these comical jokers
Whilst the King and the Kaiser
Would both be the wiser
If they travelled in Kirkburton smokers

No fear of infection
On the Kirkburton section
As you pass British Dyes on the way
For as the train passes
It pours out its gases
And drives all the microbes away

The canal with its fleet
Bringing cargoes of wheat
And of coals up to Poppleton's wharf
Bring treasures untold
And thousands of gold
Enriching the merchants - 'not 'arf'

When Deighton is passed
If you've not then been gassed
The aspect is wondrously fine
And the view of Kirkheaton
Can only be beaten
The further you get up the line

WD 2-8-0 No. 90619 approaches Highburton on 4th November, 1961.   *Geoff Lumb*

View from the railway bridge at the approach to Kirkburton station, looking towards Fenay Bridge and Huddersfield   *R. Brook Collection*

Some critics - not many
Declare that at Fenay
The loveliest view can be got
But it's pretty well certain
The one at Kirkburton
For beauty surpasses the lot

On the left and the right
A magnificent sight
Is presented for your admiration
For the view superfine
Of the North Western line
Is the one from Kirkburton station

On 15th May and 21st September, 1916 the branch was used by ambulance trains taking wounded soldiers to Huddersfield Sanatorium which was located close to the line.

Much of the branch passed through very attractive countryside, particularly after passing the industrial complex of British Dyes/ICI. Kirkheaton, Fenay Bridge and Kirkburton stations were in attractive settings, and at Kirkburton it would appear that this was enhanced by the efforts of the station staff in the tending of the station gardens. They were so successful in later years that during most of the 1920s the station gardens received awards. The year 1921 saw the station gain first prize in the LNWR North Eastern Division, whilst in 1922 the station was awarded first prize in the LNWR Northern District station garden competition, with a second prize in 1923 when the competition was continued by the LMS. In 1924 and 1926 Kirkburton again saw first prizes, this time in the LMS North Eastern District. It is also worth noting that in 1926 Thongsbridge, a nearby station on the Holmfirth branch gained 6th prize, and these were the only Yorkshire stations to gain awards. Finally in 1928 Kirkburton was awarded fifth prize in the gardens competition.

Throughout this time passenger traffic continued to be eroded. In 1921 Huddersfield Corporation Tramways purchased a fleet of 30-seater single deck motor buses with the principal objective of developing connections to the tram routes. On the 31st October that year the first of these services commenced operation to Moldgreen and Kirkheaton. In spite of this the branch timetable for July 1922 showed that the level of service remained similar to that which had prevailed throughout with 12 trains each day on weekdays, plus an extra train each way on Saturdays. The *Huddersfield Examiner* recorded a collision between a stationary Manchester Express and a motor train from Kirkburton on 30th December, 1922, although there are no more details.

The year 1923 saw the formation of the LMS, which amongst other companies included the LNWR and the L&YR. Prior to this, in 1921, Sir Arthur Walton was appointed General Manager of both the L&YR and the LNWR. Until 1922 the presence of both companies at Huddersfield was denoted by station staff wearing cap badges with the initials 'HJS' (Huddersfield Joint Station).

The 28th December, 1928 saw the retirement of a long serving employee. This was Mr W.H. Broadfield, goods foreman, who had seen 36 years service, 29 of

Kirkburton station building, the end of the line.

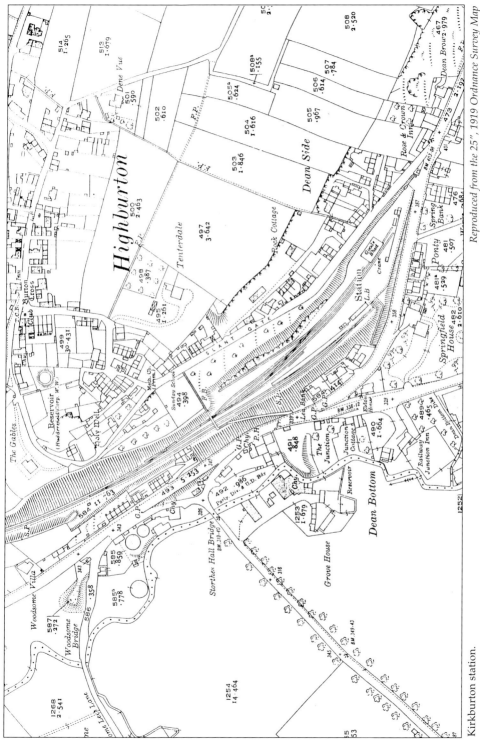

Reproduced from the 25″, 1919 Ordnance Survey Map

Kirkburton station.

A view of Kirkburton station *c.* 1910.   *Kirklees Cultural Services*

A distant view of Kirkburton station.   *R. Brook Collection*

these at Kirkburton. The presentation was undertaken by Mr J.C. Bush, who was acting station master.

Passenger services continued but on the 16th May, 1930 an agreement was entered into between Huddersfield Corporation and the London, Midland and Scottish Railway (LMS) which was to finally seal the fate of this service. On that date an agreement was entered into whereby the railway company purchased half the motor bus section of the Corporation Tramways Department and, together with the Corporation, formed the Huddersfield Joint Omnibus Committee. Each partner appointed four representatives to the committee and the agreement provided that the consent of the Joint Omnibus Committee was required before either the Corporation or the railway company could provide omnibus services within the committee's area. The General Manager of the Tramways Department at this time was Mr A.A. Blackburn MIEE, MIMechE.

On 21st February, 1992 the *Huddersfield Daily Examiner* printed an article by their transport correspondent, Mr Neil Fraser, which described a nostalgic journey on the branch. It was an intriguing description which is largely reproduced below:

Let's turn the clock back and make a sentimental journey that will bring back memories for some and for others offer a whole new experience.

We start at Huddersfield station where a Webb coal tank simmers in platform 5 on a pull and push operated train crewed by three of Huddersfield's best known railway personalities - the driver is 'Waggy' Metcalfe, the fireman Jack Jones and the guard Joe Liley.

Joe gives 'right away' and we move off, sauntering past Hillhouse sheds and slow for Kirkburton junction to make the first stop at Deighton.

On re-starting the fireman picks up the single line staff token and the train crosses Whitacre Mill viaduct, two arches of which fell down when it was first constructed.

The scenery now degenerates into what might be termed the backside of Huddersfield with an aroma to match, the bleak height of bare Dalton Bank contrasting with huge mounds of black chemical waste on either side of the line.

We go past British Dyes, through Nab Hill cutting and a moment later the atmosphere improves and the train comes to a halt at Kirkheaton. From the platform end the gradient climbs at 1 in 70.

Speed increases as we run alongside Kirkheaton ballast tip, where 4,000,000 tons of engine ash are tipped. An ear splitting shriek from the whistle gives warning to Lower Hall crossing.

Through Tandem cutting then the train thunders over Wakefield Road bridge. We go past Spa Well and Elliot's sidings, along a narrow cutting and the driver shuts the regulator to stop at Fenay Bridge and Lepton. It was here in 1884 that a passenger train collided with two gunpowder vans - without causing a single casualty.

A final re-start and we climb past Swift and Netherwoods siding and over Rowley viaduct. The last 200 yds is taken at walking pace as the engine blasts its way into the terminus from which open views reveal what a beautiful unspoilt place Kirkburton is.

LNWR locomotives were shedded at Hillhouse, which was located alongside the main line between Huddersfield and Kirkburton Junction. 2-4-0 tender engines with 5 ft diameter driving wheels and two outside cylinders, Nos. 27, 153, 314, 330, 331 and 336 were shedded there until 1880. These were replaced by 2-4-0 saddle tanks which remained until 1884, to be replaced by F.W. Webb's 2-4-2 side tanks.

As indicated earlier it appeared that the original intention had always had been to develop the branch into a through route between Huddersfield and Barnsley. With this in mind an area of land was built up between Kirkheaton and Waterloo for the development of a goods yard. Although the site was never fully developed a long siding was laid alongside the main line and this eventually split into two terminating sidings near Waterloo. The sidings were often used to hold holiday excursions and football trains in the days when Huddersfield boasted one of the best First Division teams in the country. Another frequent visitor to the sidings was the Bertram Mills circus train which tended to appear annually with an interesting variety of stock.

In view of the time since closure to regular passenger services it is inevitable that relatively few people will have memories of using the line. The following interesting comments though have been received from Mrs A. Bessy, aged 91, who still lived at Kirkheaton at the time of writing:

I was courting my husband who lived at Rowley Hill, Lepton, in the year 1914. He used to travel on the Burton train from Fenay Bridge station. He had to walk otherwise.

There were about 6 or 7 trains a day one 9.0 am, 10.0, 12 o'clock, 12.50 pm, 2.30, 3.00, 5.00, 6.00, 7.00 and one from Huddersfield at 10 o'clock. As the years went by someone else's boyfriend joined him until there were five who used to meet up to go home together. If we were going into town to the pictures the women caught the train at Kirkheaton and we all went in one carriage. There was a train at 12 o'clock at night but not for long this, no one was out so late as that.

Then comes Burton Feast and their sing in the cricket field. The train left Huddersfield about 2.00 pm and was packed when it got to Kirkheaton, there was plenty of hospitality for teas. Happy days.

He had to walk 15 minutes to Fenay Bridge station and 15 up 'Yetton' (Kirkheaton) to Moorside where I lived. When I asked if he loved me he would say, how far I come to see you and running to catch a train, I don't do it for nowt.

The author can recall his grandfather, Leonard Fisher, talking about using the train between Kirkheaton and Huddersfield when travelling to work. The author's mother, then Annie Smith, lived with her parents on Station Road, Fenay Bridge. The family took holidays in Blackpool, staying with relatives, and inevitably travelled by train. Trains from Huddersfield to Blackpool attracted large numbers of passengers, particularly at holiday times, and it was common for large queues to develop outside the station. By starting their journey at Fenay Bridge and changing at Huddersfield, the family could do some queue jumping by being already on the platform.

Chapter Seven

Industrial Connections

The Kirkburton branch was rich in industrial connections and it was these, in addition to normal goods traffic, which were instrumental in keeping the line open for many years after the regular passenger traffic ceased.

Taking a journey from Huddersfield to Kirkburton the industrial connections which could be seen and the order in which they were encountered were the Huddersfield Gasworks Railway; the Leeds Fireclay Co. Ltd; ICI Ltd, Dalton (formerly British Dyes); Elliott's Brickworks and Colliery Sidings; Victoria Colliery and a drift mine near Kirkburton station.

The Huddersfield Gasworks railway was to be seen almost immediately on leaving Huddersfield station, the main line crossing over this unique railway which opened in February 1922.

It ran from the Newtown goods yard, which was the terminus of the Midland Railway extension into Huddersfield, to the gas works on Leeds Road, with approximately a quarter of a mile of this journey being down the centre of Beaumont Street. The line also crossed Bradford and Leeds Roads and when first constructed these two main roads carried electric tram routes and the main tramway depot was immediately alongside Beaumont Street.

The line fell sharply from Newtown Yard to the gas works and this restricted trains which could be worked to a maximum of nine loaded wagons. Flagmen preceded each train on the street section. During the period 1922 to 1947 it is estimated that five million tons of coal were moved over the railway. Prior to the nationalisation of the coal industry Huddersfield Corporation painted the locomotives maroon. Under the North Eastern Gas Board, however, they were painted the standard brown used for all its vehicles. Prior to rail nationalisation the Corporation owned some 80 wagons and a steam crane from Smiths of Rodley, which was used on a works siding.

Two 0-4-0 pannier tanks with outside cylinders were used on the line. They were built by Andrew Barclay & Son Ltd of Kilmarnock and were given works numbers 1726 and 1727. The wheels and connecting rods were protected by wooden guards and the engines burnt coke to reduce smoke emission, which was particularly relevant in the street section. The railway closed in the mid-1960s.

After crossing the gasworks railway and seeing Newtown yard to the left the Hillhouse engine sheds and sidings were passed, also on the left. The next railway feature of note, this time to the right, was the sidings serving the Leeds Fire Clay Co. Limited, a brickworks situated close to Fieldhouse Lane and formerly known as Brookes Brickworks. The works had a system of sidings which were connected to the main line by a trailing point controlled from a ground frame. The main part of the sidings consisted of a steep gradient down which normal railway wagons were raised and lowered by means of a wire rope passing over revolving barrels at the side of the line. The power for this was provided by a single cylinder horizontal engine at the top of the gradient. The age and make of this engine is uncertain but it is thought that it might be

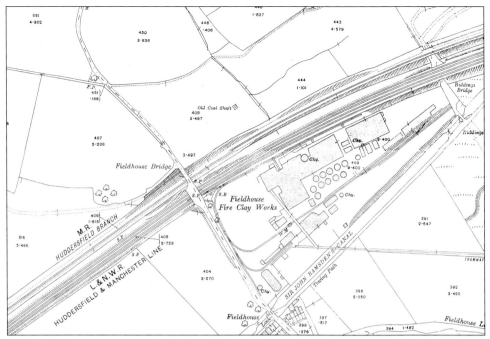

Fieldhouse Fire Clay Works.   *Reproduced from the 25″, 1919 Ordnance Survey Map*

The Fieldhouse Brickworks Horizontal Steam Engine now preserved at Tolson Memorial Museum, Huddersfield. The following is the wording on the plaque which accompanies the exhibit: 'Early Horizontal Steam Engine believed to have been built about 1850 and used at the Fieldhouse Brickworks for moving railway wagons by means of a rope. The engine was given for permanent preservation by the Leeds Fireclay Company and restored by Thomas Broadbent and Sons Limited, Engineers, Huddersfield in 1952'.   *Author*

the product of a Robert Gledhill of Bradley Mills who is known to have built such engines around 1850.

The Fieldhouse engine possessed several unusual features. It was geared to a large winding barrel which ran in a pit and the drive could be broken by sliding a pinion along the engine shaft out of mesh. This was essential as the engine could not reverse under steam and the wagons descended the gradient by gravity under the control of a foot operated band brake in the engine house. At the base of the incline the siding became level and the trucks were hauled into the centre of the works by a horse. The engine, which is now preserved at the Tolson Memorial Museum in Huddersfield, can best be described as a horizontal return connecting rod engine, the piston rod emerging from the cylinder at the opposite end from the crank which it drives through a double connecting rod passing down each side of the cylinder. It has a fly-wheel of 8 ft diameter in cast iron with four spokes, and it is thought to be one of the three oldest horizontal engines in existence. These sidings became disused shortly after 1930. As mentioned elsewhere some of the bricks used in the construction of the Whitacre Mill viaduct were manufactured at these brickworks.

Close to the junction with the branch L.B. Holliday's dyeworks had a sizeable private railway system connected to the main line but the first industrial connection on the branch proper was ICI Ltd of Dalton. This company occupies a 250 acre site which was purchased originally by Read, Holliday & Son of Bradford in 1915, when the loss of supplies from Essen Dyeworks in Germany during World War I became of national importance. This was a consequence of a derivative of dye production, picric acid, being an important constituent in the manufacture of explosives. Chemicals were first produced on the site in 1916 but, when dye production came under the control of the Ministry of Munitions Holliday became part of the newly formed British Dyes Ltd. By that time the railway had been laid into the site. The work on the new siding connection, located at the half-mile post from Kirkburton Junction, was completed on the 23rd September, 1915. On 24th September Colonel Druitt was appointed as the inspecting officer by the Board of Trade. The inspection took place on 25th November, 1915, following which Colonel Druitt wrote to the Board of Trade recommending that they sanction use. The technical comments in the letter were: points facing down trains worked from two-lever ground frame controlled by the electric train staff for the section Kirkburton Junction to Kirkheaton. On 26th November the Board of Trade wrote to the LNWR confirming that the siding connection could be used. By 1916, 45 tank wagons had been ordered from Charles Roberts Ltd of Horbury. The year 1916 also saw the provision of additional accommodation for British Dyes by the construction of crossover roads between up and down lines, plus a second platform for Deighton station. A plan showing the extent of these works is depicted elsewhere in the book. Colonel Druitt was again the inspecting officer, and following his inspection on 27th October, 1916 the Board of Trade sanctioned use of the new facilities with effect from 30th October, 1916. In 1926 the company became one of the four constituent organisations making up ICI, and specialised in the production of fine chemicals. It has always been in the forefront of new technology and was the first factory in Britain to manufacture nylon and terylene.

L.B. Hollidays private sidings 1971. It will be seen that the sidings are already closed with the main line connection having been removed.   *Author*

ICI yard: 20th March, 1963.   *F.J. Bullock*

The ICI works and its private railway. The ex-LNWR main line from Manchester to Leeds can be seen top left. Running parallel to this is Sir John Ramsden's Canal, whilst the Kirkburton branch is on the extreme right.
Reproduced from the 6", 1930 Ordnance Survey Map

ICI railway lines *c.* 1949.   *Kirklees Cultural Services*

The railway system in the works was the largest and the best private industrial railway in the district. Traffic was fed into the works from receptor sidings at Deighton on the Kirkburton branch. There was a total of seven lines, each capable of holding a train of approximately 30 wagons. The system consisted of around 20 miles of single track with 140 switches and crossings.

The track was originally constructed of 65 lb. bull-headed reversible rails, but with an increase in traffic and increased axle loading this was replaced with 85 lb. or 95 lb. rails.

In 1947, at the time of railway nationalisation, ICI possessed eight 0-4-0 saddle type shunting engines and 400 wagons of various types. Many of the wagons were used for transporting liquids and materials around the factory in addition to being used on main line trains. One of the locomotives was a 'fireless' type and this was largely used in dangerous areas where hot ashes or sparks could lead to a fire. In this type of locomotive the boiler was a steam container operating on the thermos flask principle. It could operate for approximately two hours under normal working conditions and was recharged at intervals from a central fixed steam supply.

The railway included a locomotive cleaning shed and repair shop, a wagon repair department and a qualified permanent way gang to maintain the tracks. In addition there was a breakdown van and re-railing equipment with a small gang of trained personnel always available to deal with derailments.

At the 1947 railway nationalisation the company owned the following locomotives and wagons.

Andrew Barclay, Sons & Co. Ltd, Kilmarnock: 5 in service, 35 tons gross weight each. 16 in. diameter and 24 in. stroke cylinders, 18, 900 lb. tractive effort, 550 tons hauling power on straight level track, 160 psi working pressure, 24 ft 6 in. overall length, 6 ft wheelbase. Hudswell, Clarke & Co. Ltd, Leeds: 2 in service, 28½ tons gross weight each, 14 in. diameter and 22 in. stroke cylinders, 14,500 lb. tractive effort, 400 tons hauling power on straight level track, 160 psi working pressure, 22 ft 7 in. overall length, 5 ft 6 in. wheelbase. Hawthorn, Leslie & Co. Ltd: 1 in service, 18 tons gross weight, 17 in. diameter and 16 in. stroke cylinders, 6,600 lb. tractive effort, 200 tons approximately hauling power on straight level track, 60 psi working pressure, 19 ft overall length, 5 ft 6 in. wheelbase. Tank wagons: 24 internal, 99 main line. Vans: 33 internal, Nil main line. Open wagons: 251 internal, 60 main line.

In the early 1960s the locomotive fleet was joined by a Sentinel 0-4-0 diesel shunter with a Rolls-Royce engine. A further diesel locomotive was brought to the site in 1968 and as a consequence of this steam engines were made redundant.

In 1970 the internal railway closed and the reception sidings were removed in February 1971. Right up to the time of closure a minimum of two British Rail trains per day travelled to the reception sidings and Sunday working was not unknown. At the closure several wagons were left isolated in the ICI reception sidings, these being burnt on site around December 1971 after which the scrap metal was hauled away for salvage.

Moving on down the line past Kirkheaton station Elliott's brickworks is

Former ICI locomotive No. 2226. Built by Andrew Barclay, Sons & Co. Ltd, Caledonia Works, Kilmarnock in 1946. It was used on the Huddersfield ICI internal rail system until 1967 when the traffic was taken over by diesel locomotives. It was donated by ICI to the Keighley & Worth Valley Railway in 1968 where it saw only limited use on passenger trains and was latterly kept on static display at Oxenhope Museum. In 1992 the locomotive was acquired by the Brookside Miniature Railway, Poynton, Cheshire where it is currently on static display. It was transported from the Worth Valley to Brookside on 19th June, 1992 and was subsequently painted and renamed 'Katie', after the daughter of the owner of Brookside Miniature Railway, Chris Halsall.
Author

The Kirkburton goods pulled by WD No. 90632 passing Elliot's brickworks between Kirkheaton and Fenay Bridge on 30th March, 1965. The private brickworks sidings are still in place.
F.J. Bullock

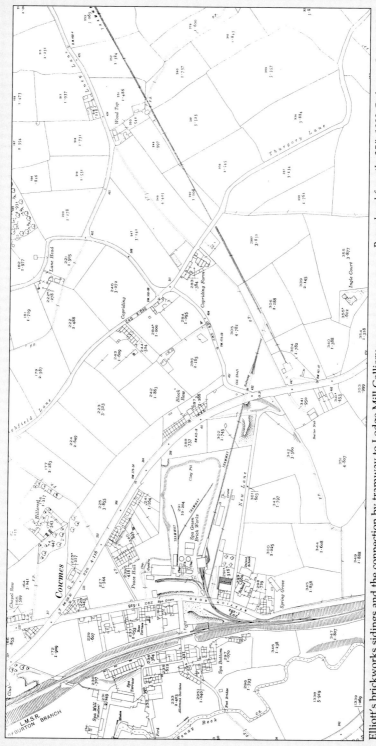

Reproduced from the 25", 1932 Ordnance Survey Map

Elliott's brickworks sidings and the connection by tramway to Lodge Mill Colliery.

Reproduced from the 25", 1919 Ordnance Survey Map

The tramway to Lodge Mill Colliery.

reached. This was, and still is, located immediately alongside the railway between Kirkheaton and Fenay Bridge and Lepton stations. Private sidings were found at this location which were opened on 25th June, 1903. The inspecting officer appointed by the Board of Trade was Col Yorke, although the actual inspection was carried out on his behalf by Colonel P.G. von Donop on 23rd June, 1903. It consisted of sidings on the down side of the single line with connections at each end and onto the running line. The points were worked by two ground frames, each of two levers locked by a key on the electric staff of the section. Owing to the gradient and the danger of vehicles running back the company undertook that the whole train would be placed on the siding before any shunting operations took place or that the engine would be at the lower end of the train. The Board of Trade agreed to the opening subject to this undertaking. According to the present brickworks management they were never used for the distribution of finished bricks but for coal. Coal was brought via a tramway from Lodge Mill, Grange Ash and Lepton Edge collieries to the sidings for distribution via the rail network.

Lodge Mill colliery closed in the 1920s but Grange Ash and Lepton Edge continued into the 1950s.

In the early days the trucks were moved around the sidings by locomotives of the railway company but this was followed by a period of horse traction and then, in later years, the trucks were shunted by a motor lorry.

Shortly after emerging from the cutting which took the line away from Fenay Bridge and Lepton station towards Kirkburton the line passed the reception sidings for Victoria Colliery which also had a connection to Woodsome Colliery. The connection to the branch was opened on the 7th December, 1905. Colonel Yorke was the Board of Trade inspecting officer. His letter recommending acceptance of the connections, following his inspection on the 5th December, 1905, indicated two connections from the ends of a loop siding, each worked from a ground frame containing two levers locked by a key on the electric train staff. Due to the gradient all trains working at the siding had to have the engine at the lower end. Emerging from the loop were the colliery lines which radiated into a spread of eight loops and one dead-end siding. They were connected to the colliery and drifts further up the hillside by a self-acting tramway incline. In the 1920s Smith and Netherwood, the owners of the mine, were despatching an average of 40 wagons per day. During World War II the owners were Huddersfield Collieries and the output was slightly increased. The mine never became part of the National Coal Board but it did continue as a licensed mine closing in the 1960s, the final owners being Lepton Coal and Clay Co.

The final industrial connection was seen just before Kirkburton station where a drift mine emerged adjacent to the tracks but just above track level. The local parlance for a drift mine was 'day hole'. The mine was worked for many years by a firm called Sykes. It was excavated into the side of the railway cutting and wooden staging at the entrance gave access and provided a platform for the loading of coal into railway wagons on a specially constructed siding.

Reproduced from the 25", 1919 Ordnance Survey Map

Victoria Colliery, its reception sidings and tramway.

Chapter Eight

Closure to Passengers

The branch closed to passengers on Saturday the 26th July, 1930. The closure was recorded in the *Huddersfield Daily Examiner* of the 28th July, from which article the following information is taken.

After 61 years of continuous service the passenger train service, which has operated over the Kirkburton branch line from Huddersfield since 1869, came to an end on Saturday evening with the running of the 10.47 from Huddersfield.

Keen competition from the buses brought the railway company to the decision to terminate the service on the line connecting Huddersfield with Deighton, Kirkheaton, Fenay Bridge and Kirkburton. The buses gained the advantage over the trains largely as the result of a large loop having to be made to take in the first two stations. The trains take 18 minutes to make the journey. Similar branch lines are being closed in other parts of the country where they are not a paying proposition.

When the line was first built it was intended to take it through to the West Riding collieries, but this idea was abandoned with the opening of the Huddersfield to Penistone line in the 1850s.

The Kirkburton line will continue to be used for excursion trains and for goods traffic. Parcels, luggage, fish, newspapers etc., consigned for various stations on the line will, however, be delivered from Huddersfield by motor van.

The article was accompanied by a photograph bearing the caption 'Journey's End'.

Although the article indicated that the advantage gained by buses was due to the large loop at the beginning of the journey, a further major drawback had been that the stations were in the valley bottom whereas the villages they served were well up the hill slopes meaning that lengthy walks were involved for the majority of passengers. Throughout the life of the branch passenger services had become increasingly vulnerable to competition from road vehicles, commencing with the steam trams. As indicated earlier in the book, the final death knell appeared to come some two months prior to the withdrawal of the passenger service when an agreement was entered into between the LMS and the Huddersfield Corporation Tramways Department to form the Huddersfield Joint Omnibus Committee.

It is difficult to assess what impact the closure had on local people but the information available would suggest that it was very little. Compared to the official opening the closure warranted scant mention in the local press and no reference was made to any potential hardships.

On 9th August, 1930, less than one month after the withdrawal of the passenger service, an article appeared in the *Huddersfield Examiner* about Kirkburton, and this included the following reference to the railway:

Although it is several miles from Huddersfield and among real 'country' Kirkburton is not an 'out of the way' village. True, the railway service which it has enjoyed to the extent of ten trains per day to and from Huddersfield (with three trains extra each way on Saturdays and with none at all on Sundays) for a number of years has just been discontinued, but that is only because the numerous buses which pass through the village have transformed it more or less into a 'suburb of Huddersfield' and made it unnecessary to run trains as well. The train service was begun in 1869 [sic].

Ex-L&YR 2-4-2T No. 50865 is seen near the footbridge on the approach to Kirkburton station as it runs round its train on the occasion of a tour of local lines organised by the Stephenson Locomotive Society and the Manchester Locomotive Society on 5th May, 1951.   R. Brook

Chapter Nine

Total Closure

In spite of losing its regular passenger services at a comparatively early date the branch remained open throughout its length for goods traffic for a further 35 years and a short section remained open for 6 years beyond that to serve the ICI.

As was noted in the previous chapter, after the cessation of passenger services parcels and similar traffic were conveyed from Huddersfield by road transport. Most of the industrial connections remained in use, however, and full truck loads of coal continued to be handled at all the stations along the line.

In addition the goods facilities at Kirkheaton were widely used by local mills bringing coal and wool inwards and woollen piece goods outwards. In later years the station was also a receiving point for pit props which were then conveyed onwards by National Coal Board lorries. As mentioned earlier the sidings at Fenay Bridge and Lepton station were used for gunpowder traffic for nearby fireworks factories.

The Kirkburton branch and the railway scene in general experienced many changes during the period that the branch was open for goods traffic only. In 1937 a degree of remodelling took place on the branch in favour of goods only operation. In particular the junction with the main line was relaid for the benefit of block chemical trains and a speed limit of 20 mph was imposed. The branch was operated on the basis of 'one engine in steam'. After a gradual demise over a period of years the use of railway horses for road cartage was discontinued at Huddersfield during 1951. A number of horses were purchased by the Blue Cross League and retired to the country, whilst the drays or lorries were gathered at the Newtown goods yard and offered for sale to farmers etc. In 1958 colour light signalling at Huddersfield was introduced, which entailed the closure of two manual signal boxes and their replacement by a single building on the island platform. The year 1960 brought the reprieve of the Kirkburton branch beyond Kirkheaton as an unstaffed line used only for the working of full truckloads of coal to Kirkburton.

Although closed to regular passenger services the branch continued to be used on occasion for excursions and special trains. Specially booked excursions travelled to destinations such as Doncaster Races, Blackpool and Llandudno. The 24th September, 1943 saw the exhibition of an American locomotive in the goods yard at Kirkburton station. This was undertaken as part of a 'Spotlight on America' programme organised by the Kirkburton 'Service of Youth' Council. On 5th May, 1951 a Pennine Rail Tour was organised by the Stephenson Locomotive Society in conjunction with the Manchester Locomotive Society using an ex-L&YR 2-4-2T No. 50865 pulling four corridor coaches. This visited several local branches in the area, including Kirkburton. The 1950s also saw a number of football specials being stored on the branch whilst the game was in progress. One in particular is recalled from a Huddersfield Town versus Tottenham Hotspur match which consisted of a

Kirkburton station building is in a rather dilapidated condition as ex-L&YR 2-4-2T No. 50865 prepares ready to run round its train on 5th May, 1951.   *R. Brook*

British Railways 'Standard' 2-6-4T No. 80044 seen on 2nd May, 1959 on a special at the approach to Kirkburton station.   *G.W. Morrison*

General view of Kirkburton with Railway Enthusiasts Club special ready to leave with No.
80044 on 2nd May, 1959.   *G.W. Morrison*

WD 2-8-0 No. 90619 arrives at Kirkburton with a goods train on 4th November, 1961.
                                                                          Geoff Lumb

Deighton: 20th March, 1963. The train has just left the Whitacre Mill viaduct heading towards Huddersfield. It will soon be passing through the remains of Deighton station.   *F.J. Bullock*

Kirkheaton yard: 20th March, 1963.   *F.J. Bullock*

Kirkburton station: 20th March, 1963. The passenger station building can still be seen on the right although the track into the station has now been lifted.   *F.J. Bullock*

Railway Correspondence and Travel Society special near Kirkburton on 6th September, 1964. This is close to closure and shows the overgrown condition of the track and how some lines have already been removed. *Geoff Lumb*

The approach to Kirkburton on 6th September, 1964 with a Railway Correspondence and Travel Society special.

WD 2-8-0 No. 90362 passes near the ICI works with the Kirkburton goods on 30th March, 1965.
F.J. Bullock

WD 2-8-0 No. 90362 at Kirkburton on 30th March, 1965, just a few days before total closure of this section of the line.
F.J. Bullock

class 'B17' 4-6-0 with 10 coaches. A number of other specials were organised on the line by interested groups, including the Railway Enthusiasts Club on 2nd May, 1959 and the Railway Correspondence and Travel Society on 6th September, 1964, but otherwise the traffic consisted of a daily goods train carrying coal, pit props and general merchandise plus the ICI trains using the first part of the branch.

With increasing competition goods traffic declined until on 5th April, 1965 goods facilities were removed from all the stations and track lifting commenced the following year, with the exception of that section which served the ICI. An article in the *Huddersfield Daily Examiner* for Friday, 26th August ,1966, under the heading 'It's the end of the line for "Kirkburton Dick"', recorded that one year short of its century the greater part of the Kirkburton branch railway was being demolished and with it a colourful chapter in local history was being concluded.

The last remaining section of the branch, from Kirkburton Junction, through the remains of Deighton station, over Whitacre Mill viaduct to the ICI works, a distance of approximately one mile, continued to provide rail connections to the ICI sidings for a further six years, but this finally succumbed to closure in February 1971.

English Electric type '3' Co-Co No. D6937 passing through the remains of Deighton station on 7th September, 1968. This was the only section of line remaining open for traffic to the ICI. The remaining platform was built in 1916. The original platform can just be traced on the left. Interesting to note that although the rail connection has gone the yard is still being used by a coal merchant.   *G.W. Morrison*

Demolition of the road bridge near Kirkheaton station *c.* 1973. Note the advertisement for Belle Vue, near Manchester, which has also subsequently closed. *Huddersfield Examiner*

Footbridge near Kirkburton station still in place in 1973, but the railway is long gone and replaced by a garden to the housing estate now on the site. *Huddersfield Examiner*

Postscript

And so what of the line since closure. Whilst the course of the line can be followed for much of its route the railway character tends to be gradually diminished as time passes. Bridges which carried the railway over roads have been demolished but the two viaducts have survived almost intact. The station site at Deighton was used for the construction of a banana warehouse in 1972 whilst the goods yard is used by a timber merchant. Kirkheaton station site has been redeveloped for light industry and the Kirkburton station site and the track bed as far as the footbridge was developed for housing in 1971/72, the site being called Northwood Park. The old footbridge itself was demolished in 1980 following complaints from residents in the new houses. The ends of the path were blocked off on Friday and demolition started on the Monday, the demolition going ahead in spite of a massive campaign by the Civic Society, who established that it had been constructed to preserve a right of way. Kirklees Council were approached by the Civic Society but refused to spot list the bridge and it was some two years before the footpath link was restored, this time at ground level. The station site at Fenay Bridge remains undeveloped and is still used by a coal merchant as in the railway days. The platform is still visible although the buildings were demolished whilst the line was still open for goods traffic.

The future of the Kirkburton branch as a transportation route was considered by the then West Yorkshire Passenger Transport Committee in January 1977, the following information being taken from a report which appeared in the *Huddersfield Examiner* on 27th January, 1977.

A Wakefield meeting heard the previous day that two disused local railway lines could be used by other means of transport, but that a third was to be retained just in case it was needed.

The lines rejected by the West Yorkshire Passenger Transport Committee were the Kirkburton branch line and the Mirfield to Heckmondwike line. The committee decided to accept a sub-committee recommendation to keep their options open on the line from Huddersfield to Brighouse and Norwood Green.

With regard to the Kirkburton branch the committee recommended that the line south of the ICI Dalton Works should be turned over to use as a bridleway, busway, footpath, cycleway or road.

Interest in the branch was again aroused on 26th April, 1982 when a new station at Deighton was opened. It was constructed adjacent to the site of the former Deighton station, access being obtained from the Whitacre Street road bridge, as previously, but from the opposite side of the road. The platform is virtually on the site of the Kirkburton branch junction. The official opening took place in the morning and the *Huddersfield Examiner* of Monday 26th April, 1982 reported that Kirklees Mayor, Councillor Fred Pickles, rode in on the footplate of a special six-car train to open the Deighton rail station.

Councillor Pickles, a train driver, was watched by 250 local schoolchildren waiting to clamber aboard the train for a trip to Leeds and back.

The station cost £65,000 to build and it was one of nine new stations to be opened during the following three years under the Metrotrain scheme run by the West Yorkshire Passenger Transport Executive in collaboration with British Rail.

Opening of the new Deighton station on 26th April, 1982. The left-hand platform is located
approximately on the site of the former Kirkburton Junction. *F.J. Bullock*

The PTE's Director General, Mr Robin Ward, said that 'the opening of the Deighton station is another important milestone in the history of public transport in West Yorkshire. We are confident that it will benefit the local community and provide the opportunity for a more efficient travel interchange'.

At the time of the opening over 70 trains a day called at the station, running between Leeds, Huddersfield and Manchester and between Huddersfield and Wakefield, although there was only a limited service on Sundays.

Traffic forecasts were based on there being more than 1,250 homes within a 10 minute walk of the station plus a large industrial area nearby on Leeds Road. It was anticipated that the station would attract 500 to 600 passengers a day.

And so after 52 years Deighton again had a railway station. It is particularly interesting to note the number of trains stopping at the station on a daily basis compared to the original Deighton station, plus a limited Sunday service, which was never the case with the Kirkburton branch.

In regard to the future of the trackbed beyond ICI to Kirkburton the local Planning Officer has advised that the line has been protected in part through provision in village plans as a route for a footpath. The individual village plans will be replaced by a comprehensive unitary development plan for Kirklees, the draft of which has been endorsed by council, and this takes an overall view of the branch line with a proposal to create a strategic cycleway and footpath. Unfortunately the track bed is not complete, with major blockages at Fenay Bridge and Waterloo, which will necessitate the creation of alternative routes. The unitary development plan is subject to public consultation.

Whilst the opening of a new station at Deighton recreated the opportunity to travel the first section of what was the journey to Kirkburton there is also currently a proposal which could result in the relaying of the first nine furlongs of the branch to enable ICI Organics to convey bulk train loads to the works. A private Parliamentary Bill has been prepared by the company for opening this section of the line for freight purposes, and details of this Bill have been deposited with the local authorities legal service for public inspection.

And so in spite of the early loss of a passenger service from this branch the final chapter may well not have been written and it is just possible that at least a section of the line could again provide some service which will be of benefit to the local economy.

Bibliography

The Place Names of the West Riding of Yorkshire, F.W. Moorman, Thoresby Society, Leeds, 1910.

West Riding of Yorkshire, Arthur Raistrick, Hodder and Stoughton, 1970.

The Leeds, Huddersfield and Manchester Railway: The Standedge Line, Martin Bairstow, Halifax, 1984.

The Mining and Quarrying Industries in the Huddersfield District, D.H. Holmes BSc., Tolson Memorial Museum, Huddersfield, 1967.

Pennine Journey, William Stocks, Advertiser Press, Huddersfield, 1960.

A Regional History of the Railways of Great Britain, Vol. 8 South and West Yorkshire, David Joy, David & Charles, Newton Abbot, 1975.

A Scrapbook of Huddersfield, Noel Spencer, Kirklees Metropolitan Council, 1990.

Bradshaw's Railway Guides.

Urban District of Kirkburton, Official Handbook.

Minute Books: Kirkburton Local Board.

Parkins Almanac.

Kirkburton Civic Society, Robert A. Carter.

Huddersfield Examiner.

Huddersfield Chronicle.

Leeds Mercury.

Ordnance Survey maps.

Files of the Public Record Office, Kew.

'The Three Owls' public house, close to the site of Kirkburton station. Originally called the 'Railway Junction Inn', possibly in anticipation of a proposal in 1864 by the Midland Railway to construct an extension from Barnsley to a junction with the LNWR at Kirkburton. *Author*